CONCILIUM

Jesus said, 'Suffer the little children to come to me and forbid them not,
for theirs is the kingdom of heaven' (Matt. 19. 14)

Suffer the little children . . .
Little children suffer.

concilium 1996/2

LITTLE CHILDREN SUFFER

Edited by

Maureen Junker-Kenny and
Norbert Mette

SCM Press · London
Orbis Books · Maryknoll

Published by SCM Press Ltd, 9–17 St Albans Place, London N1
and by Orbis Books, Maryknoll, NY 10545

ISBN: 0 334 03037 4 (UK)
ISBN: 1 57075 071 8 (USA)

Typeset at The Spartan Press Ltd, Lymington, Hants
Printed by Mackays of Chatham, Kent

Concilium Published February, April, June, August, October, December.

Contents

Editorial: Little Children Suffer – The Child in the Midst

'And he took a child, and put it in the midst of them' (Mark 9.36 par.). Today, as in the time of Jesus, this scene, sparked off by the dispute among the disciples as to who was the greatest, is a tremendous provocation. Jesus explains to his ambitious followers that children, not adults, are first in line for the kingdom of God. When in addition to this we remember the connotations of 'being in the midst' in a Jewish context (where this important place is reserved for the Torah), the explosive force of this demonstrative gesture on the part of Jesus will be obvious. Nor is there any indication of anything special about the child which Jesus thought worthy to put in the midst. He probably took the nearest child – boy or girl, we do not know.

So in the eyes of Jesus children are heralds and representatives of that kingly rule of God which has already dawned for them. Taking this seriously entails a series of consequences for discipleship of Jesus. The principle for the way in which the church and the local Christian community deals with children must not be that the church makes them children of God, but that they are children of God already. In that way children will constantly and lastingly be reminded that the kingdom of God is greater than the church. A study by the British Council of Churches on *The Child in the Church* says that 'children are a gift to the church'. By way of explanation the text adds: 'The Lord of the church sets them in the midst of the church, today as in Galilee, not as objects of benevolence, nor even as recipients of instruction, but in the last analysis as patterns of discipleship. The church that does not accept children unconditionally into its fellowship is depriving those children of what is theirs rightfully, but the deprivation such a church will itself suffer is far more grave.'[1]

To allow children to share in the experience of unconditional acceptance (cf. Mark 10.13–16 par.) is far from being the childishly simple matter it might look at first sight. It represents first and foremost a fundamental shift of standpoint and perspective, beginning with the concern to see ourselves as adults and our environment with the eyes of children, i.e. 'from below', and extending to an examination of the current way of looking at childhood. Is the state of our society such that children can really feel accepted and well in it? Don't they often feel more or less vividly that there is basically no place for them or, if there is one, that it is at best on the periphery? And at the latest when they leave the niches and reserves arranged for them by education, they are regarded as a burdensome disruption to the peace. One can treat them as one likes, since they are not yet persons in their own right; they still have to grow up. That is a view which continues to be widespread and which in addition allows the marginalization that is actually practised to seem justified.

One of the paradoxes of more recent history is that on the one hand the 'discovery of childhood' is bound up with the rise and development of modernity,[2] yet on the other it is precisely these children who feel most persistently and most painfully the consequences of the process of modernization which is increasingly accelerating. Particularly in our day we can note to a terrifying degree how children have to grow up without experiencing childhood – even in prosperous societies; and this situation seems to be increasing rather than decreasing. The first four contributions to this issue indicate that this estimate is anything but excessively pessimistic. Sometimes in surveys, and sometimes through case studies (on the one hand for the so-called 'Third World' and on the other for prosperous societies), they report on and analyse the situation of children today – at the end of the century that Ellen Key had optimistically believed she could describe as the 'century of the child'.

That is not, however, to say that Ellen Key and other educationalists, who sparked off a notable reform movement in theory and practice at the beginning of this century, have failed in their passionate concern for the dignity and rights of children. They provided decisive stimuli to research into childhood which has opened up a new perspective on this phase of life – as an independent mode of being human. In particular, it has become clear that from the beginning children have taken an active part in shaping their development, and in this sense are subjects who form themselves. But at the same time, in this process they are dependent on intensive reciprocation from adults, the reinforcement and protection of their possiblities for development. This paradox, which according to Schleiermacher characterizes being human generally, as the twofold constitution of being independent and dependent, is evident to a heightened degree in childhood and explains the special vulnerability of children. The conditions in family and society in which children must or may grow up need to be noted urgently by educationalists, and in some countries – in this issue there is an example from the USA – have recently become the subject of cultural debates. However, the problem in implementing the structural measures which would have to be taken here remains that children have difficulties in finding a political lobby.

Aren't special demands made here on a church which has received and has to hand on the good news of the unconditional acceptance of children? But if these demands are to be met, it is necessary for more consistent attention to be paid to children; within the church, too, they need to be seen as subjects with full rights – in faith as well. This is, after all, how Jesus treated them. The articles in the second part of this issue seek to contribute to this by developing some of the central facets of the view of the child as subject (in connection with developmental psychology, the Bible, dogma and educational theory).[3]

Finally, the articles in the third part are concerned to reflect on the practical consequences of this and to give examples. Here attention is drawn explicitly to the special responsibility of the church to be an advocate of children – from dealing with them in its own spheres of action, including liturgy and church law, to resolute commitment to a society in which children no longer have to live out a marginal existence but find their place in the midst of it. The reports of work with children who have had to experience and suffer the fact of being quite simply excluded from society are particularly impressive – and challenging – here.[4] Here it becomes especially evident what happens and can happen if there is a consistent attempt to put into the practice the theological formula that 'salvation and God are only where children can also be',[5] in other words, if the children who live with us are put in our midst.[6]

Maureen Junker-Kenny
Norbert Mette

Notes

1. British Council of Churches, *The Child in the Church*, 1976, 17f.
2. Cf. especially P. Ariès, *Centuries of Childhood*, London 1962.
3. For this change of perspective see the document produced by the Synod of the Evangelical Church in Germany, *Aufwachsen in schwieriger Zeit. Kinder in Gemeinde und Gesellschaft*, Gütersloh 1995.
4. In connection with the planning for this volume, F. Heselaars Hartono SJ

compiled an extensive and very interesting piece of documentation on church work with street children (*anak jalanan*) in Indonesia. This can be sent on request.

5. Here quoted from H. Braun, 'Markus 10, 13–18', *Göttinger Predigtmeditationen* 17, 1962/63, 258–62: 260.

6. Cf. also the basic working document of the Brazilian Conference of Bishops on the 'Brotherhood Campaign 1987', 'Whoever accepts a child, accepts me', São Paulo 1986.

I · The Situation of Children Today

Not a 'Century of the Child' – the Situation of Children in the World in the 1990s

Norbert Mette

In 1890 Ellen Key, the Swedish educational reformer and pioneer in the women's movement, programmatically entitled the dawn of a new era which she thought possible and imminent 'the century of the child'. What has become of it – more than 100 years later? Unfortunately a contribution on the topic promised for this issue has failed to arrive. So we have to approach it in a different way. Year by year, UNICEF presents a report on 'The Situation of Children in the World'. Here I shall show how this has changed between 1991 and 1996. The picture is ambivalent: concern for the interests of children has grown, but we are still far from a 'century of the child'. A series of noteworthy documents indicates the learning process which has begun here in some churches. Three are particularly important:

British Council of Chuches, *The Child in the Church*, 1979
National Council of the Bishops of Brazil, *Com acolhe o Menor, a Mimi acolhe. A Fraternidade e o Menor*, 1987
Synod of the Evangelical Church in Germany, *Aufwachsen in schwieriger Zeit. Kinder in Gemeinde und Gesellschaft*, 1994

But now to what UNICEF reported.

1991

UNICEF noted that the World Summit for Children was particularly marked by two problems. First was the fact that 40,000 children die every day from malnutrition and quite common illnesses, 150 million children have to fight with damaged health and disrupted growth, and 100 million children between six and eleven years of age do not go to school. Secondly, there are now the technical organizational and financial means for ending this silent catastrophe. Large-scale studies and researches in many countries have helped the world to be in a better position than ever not only to recognize many problems but also to solve them. So the key question for the Summit was whether human ethics can keep up with these new possibilities. In the future will all be done that could be done?

In the developing countries, at the present time it is estimated that 14 million children under the age of five die every year – more than 250,000 a week. The direct causes of more than 60% of these deaths can be counted on the fingers of one hand: diarrhoea, measles, tetanus, whooping cough and inflammation of the lungs. All these diseases could be avoided or treated today at minimal cost. Many children in Africa and Latin America are still paying a high price for the indebtedness of their countries in the form of declining family income and continued savings in the areas of health and education; they pay for this with disruptions to growth, reduced opportunities for education and often enough with their lives.

In the year 2000 the principle 'children first' would mean that the chances of a child surviving to adulthood, growing up mentally and physically intact, having enough to eat, being given medical care, being vaccinated at the right time and going to school would no longer be affected by factors like the balance of payments, the interest-rate level, the favourable or unfavourable development of trading conditions, the electoral victory of a particular party, or others of the many unavoidable vicissitudes which shape adult life. But even the industrialized nations are far from having implemented the principle 'children first'. Although the 1980s generally brought increasing prosperity, for millions of children in some of the richest societies of earth they were a 'lost decade'. In the last ten years the proportion of children living below the official levels of poverty in their countries has increased in almost all Western countries, thus e.g. in Germany, Great Britain, Ireland, Canada and the USA.

1992

In general, so little note is taken of the effects of the wrong decisions and excesses of the adult world on children that even now there are in practice no mechanisms for gaining precise information about the levels of nourishment of children, their proneness to illness and school attendance. Even in times of social upheaval in which experience shows children in particular to be exposed to the greatest risks, it is simpler to discover how many VCRs have been imported each month than to gain precise information about the state of health and nourishment of children in a country.

In normal circumstances girls by nature have a better chance of surviving the first particularly risky years of life. However, circumstances in the developing countries are not normal. In many countries of southern Asia more boys survive than girls. Discrimination (against the female sex) can be measured by this gap between the natural and the actual chances of survival. In Bangladesh, India and Pakistan it results in more than a million deaths a year. In other words, a million girls die there every year simply because they did not come into the world as boys. In the developing countries today more boys are learning to read and write than girls. In some countries boys are brought to health centres more than twice as often as girls. Whether in the workplace, in social welfare, before the law, in matters of property or even in civil rights and political freedoms, human rights and freedoms always depend on the chance existence of one chromosome.

There are many external reasons for ongoing poverty, but indisputably one of the main ones is the fact that usually no start in life is made possible for the children of poor families which allows them even to use the chances that are there. So one of the main aims of any development must be to break through this 'internal' vicious circle which begins with the hindrance to mental and physical growth through malnutrition and sickness and which in turn leads to bad results in school and at work; this continues in adults whose capacity to earn a living, to stimulate change and react to new opportunities are hampered; in the end it results in poor families which are often too big, which are prone to malnutrition and illness, and thus carry on the wave of poverty from one generation to the next.

1995

Between 1950 and 1990 the average expectation of life increased from around forty to sixty-two years. Child mortality has declined by two-thirds from around 300 to 100 births per thousand. The illiteracy rate has doubled world-wide and now is almost 40%. Smallpox, from which up to 5 million people died annually in the early 1950s, has now been eradicated. Polio, measles, malnutrition, deficiencies in vitamins and trace elements, and diarrhoea are being effectively fought against. All in all, according to the World Bank in its 1993 report, 'worldwide, health conditions have steadily improved over the last forty years to a greater degree than in the whole of previous world history'.

1996

Of course there is a concern for children to be brought up healthily and develop normally. Of course it is possible to overcome absolute poverty. Of course the population growth can be slowed down. Of course the pollution of the environment can be stopped. For decades the decisive question in all these problems has not been what is possible but what the priorities are. Indeed, all these problems could largely have been solved already in the 1970s and 1980s. If only a tenth of the resources employed in these two decades for world-wide armament had been put at the disposal of the most important development areas, our world today would look quite different. There would be virtually no malnutrition; diseases and handicaps would have been drastically reduced; the literacy rate and the level of education would be considerably higher; incomes would have risen and birth rates dropped; there would be fewer social and ecological problems, fewer civil wars, fewer refugees and fewer international conflicts.

Modern methods of warfare have considerably increased the dangers for children. It is estimated that during the 1980s:
– 2 million children were killed;
– 4 to 5 million children were crippled;
– 12 million children were driven from their homeland;
– more than 1 million children lost their parents or were separated from them
– 10 million children were psychologically traumatized.

Most children who die in times of war are not hit by bombs or bullets, but fall victim to hunger or disease. Thus in Somalia in 1992 more than half the children under the age of five died. Around 90% of them fell victim to a fatal interaction of disease and malnutrition.

Millions of children have experiences which are far more terrible than the worst nightmares of adults. In Sarajevo, where almost one child in four has been wounded in the war, UNICEF carried out an investigation of 1505 children in the summer of 1993. It proved that 97% of the children had experienced grenade explosions at close quarters, 29% felt 'intolerable suffering' and 20% had nightmares. Around 55% had been shot at by snipers, and 66% had already once been close to death.

And open warfare is only part of the world-wide violence against children. In the streets of the world's cities, from Los Angeles through São

Paulo to Manila, millions of children are fighting for survival in 'battlefield conditions'. Pistols, knives and fights with the police or military or even among one another are part of their brutal everyday life. In the USA violent gangs, often in areas where drugs are prevalent, are attracting younger and younger children. In some Latin American cities businessmen pay policemen in their spare time, guards or even contract killers to do away with street children.

The Convention on the Rights of the Child has already proved a stable framework for international activities. As it has already been recognized by 178 countries, a world-wide ratification is in sight. Now the aim must be to implement it. All countries are called on to fulfil at least the basic obligations which go with ratification.

The Convention lays down the social and economic rights of children: the right to survival, to undisturbed development in early childhood, school education, health care and humane and dignified living conditions. But it also includes civil rights and political rights. These include the right of the child to a name and a citizenship, to freedom of speech, to a participation in decisions about its welfare, to protection from discrimination on grounds of race, sex or minority status, and from all forms of sexual or other exploitation. However, the important progress lies in the recognition of the child as an independent individual. The Convention prescribes that the child has its own identity, different from its parents and those who bring it up, and that the community has the duty to protect this identity and make it possible for the child to assert itself in questions like guardianship or custody rights.

It is amazing how important the topic of children has become in politics and public affairs over the last decade. Most leading politicians in fact take it seriously today. The interests of children are now on the political agenda everywhere both in the industrial nations and in the developing countries, and play a role in media reports which can no longer be overlooked. The World Summit for Children in 1990 and the acceptance of the Convention on the Rights of the Child are symbols of this new status and have contributed towards ensuring a firm place for children and young people in political and social discussions.

The public interest in children which has grown up sees them not only as 'citizens most in need of protection' but also as the 'most valuable resource of humankind' or as a demographic sub-group which is numerically interesting. Children are now seen in their own right. Processes of modernization and urbanization lasting over decades have not only improved children's chances of survival and development but also changed attitudes to children and young people. Parents expect more for their children – and also from their children – than they used to. And society, too, invests more in their education and training.

All this justifies hopes for the future of children – there is no occasion for despair. The successes which have been achieved in the last fifty years justify belief that despite war and poverty the world will no longer leave its children in the lurch, marginalize them or treat them as of no account.

It has been a long struggle to get children to be taken seriously. It took half a century to get children put at the centre of programmes of international development and human rights. But now they have their place there and nothing will drive them from it. Therefore even in view of all the conflicts and deprivations, it can be said that now the twenty-first century will belong to the children, that century which Ellen Key had hoped for more than one hundred years ago. So the most important task is to shape politics, aid programmes, basic principles and finance so that they also in practice take account of the rising status of children.

Translated by John Bowden

Being a Child in Central Africa Today Between 'tradition' and 'modernity'

Emmanuel Ntakarutimana

The whole world will have been shocked by the pictures of the unaccompanied or orphan children who were survivors of the dramatic massacres in Central Africa in 1990.[1] The psychological traumas suffered by these children will leave deep traces and have consequences on their social life which are difficult to foresee. This drama is all the more profound because it destructures the anthropological view which had contributed to the coherence of the social groups in the region. For us, to reflect on the child in fact amounts to asking ourselves about the image of men and women which society would want to have of them as a social group.

In the traditional societies of central Africa, social organization was founded on alliances of families, on clans, ethnic groups or tribes. As social partners claimed the same ancestor or lived in some form of alliance, the ties generated by these came to assume capital importance. It was in this environment that the child found its place in culture and appropriate cultural symbols and values. This tradition was still far from the present-day school which aims at handing down knowledge and techniques by 'teachers foreign to the family', without necessarily being an initiation into the art and wisdom of living.

In this article I want to sketch out a picture of cultural anthropology as it brought the child to maturity and coming of age. This will allow us to have a better appreciation of the crisis which has marked the area of the Great Lakes in Africa as a confrontation between two epistemological heritages which have yet to be reconciled, one which handed down tradition with a basic preoccupation of seeking harmony and one which has launched a massive invasion of present-day society as a confrontation with reality under the forms of mastery and domination.

I Traditional thought as a symbolic universe with which everything is in solidarity

An attentive observer of traditional milieux will quickly note that everything is 'legion'. Every object, every being, every plant, every tree, every forest is inhabited by a network of forces. Contact with each of these can be the occasion for an increase or decrease in vital force. There is an interconnection of things which means that all must secure the benevolence of their environment, visible or invisible, material or immaterial. This led to a refined series of 'fetishes' and to a whole symbolic ritual integrating the biological, the physiological, the spiritual and the communal, depending on the different circumstances which marked the life of individuals and communities.

1. The life-cycle
The table reproduced opposite[2] brings together the different transitions in human life.

2. Rites of passage and progressive integration
Between being a foetus and coming of age the child passes through stages which are codified symbolically. Conception by the mother can be accompanied with prophylactic rites, prohibitions of place, food, drink and company. All this will be determined by the ancestor of whom the child is thought to be the replica or by the social environment of the time. The mother can wear symbolic objects (bracelets, rings, 'fetishes', etc.), which concentrate the prophylactic forces. Throughout the period of pregnancy a local wise woman will provide advice and appropriate therapy, both physiological and psycho-social.

Birth is a period of the delivery and liberation of the vital force which gives rise to family rejoicing and social rejoicing. From this moment on, a whole ritual will be followed to mark the period of the mother's post-natal seclusion. The healing of the child's umbilical cord is marked by a ritual of recovery and purification which allows the mother to resume ordinary work. On this occasion the grandmother, aunt or father cuts the hair with which the child came into the world. This can even correspond to a rite which consists in taking the child through the village either on someone's back or in a basket (especially in the case of twins), to the rhythm of songs and dances.

The ceremony of giving a name, performed by the other children in the village and the nuclear family, is also an occasion for gathering the clan and

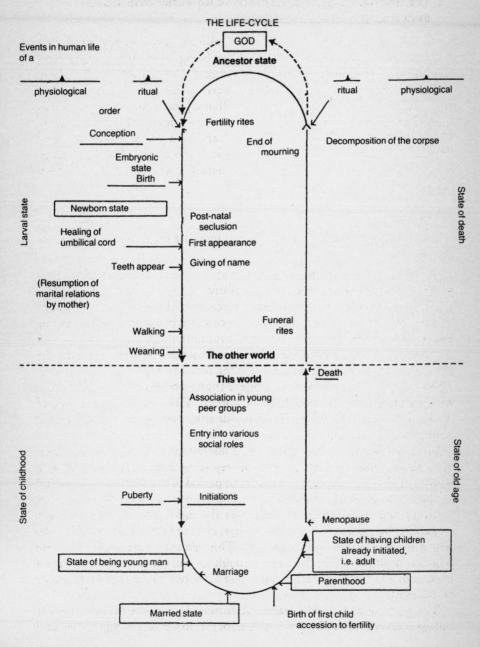

THE LIFE-CYCLE

Events in human life
of a

physiological   ritual   ritual   physiological

order

Conception   Fertility rites

End of
mourning   Decomposition of the corpse

Embryonic
state
Birth

Newborn state   Post-natal
seclusion

Healing of
umbilical cord   First appearance

Teeth appear   Giving of name

(Resumption of
marital relations
by mother)

Walking   Funeral
rites

Weaning   The other world

Larval state

State of death

GOD
Ancestor state

Death

This world

Association in young
peer groups

Entry into various
social roles

Puberty   Initiations

State of childhood

State of old age

Menopause

State of having children
already initiated,
i.e. adult

State of being young man   Marriage

Parenthood

Married state   Birth of first child
accession to fertility

Adulthood

the neighbours. The names are always highly significant and sum up the whole social and historical context of the birth of the child. This is why, for example, the tradition of family names which people tried to import into Burundi with colonization and the first evangelization did not take root. Each person had to have his or her name, since this was the concentration of a history which had to be deciphered. There were names involved with predestination, as for twins and those who came after twins. The names even became ways of tricking destiny, above all among those who had experienced many deaths. 'Evil sounding names' and 'spectral names' were supposed to keep death away from 'a being who is worthless'. By contrast, brave names were meant to lead the child to recapitulate all the bravery of his ancestors.

The emergence of the first tooth shows that the child is moving towards being free from dependence on its mother's milk; this allows parents to resume conjugal relations and makes a new conception possible. This is the period of weaning. The child who had up till then developed in the undifferentiated world of its mother's breast and in a relationship reduced to its mother's universe, has to confront a universe open to the wider family and to neighbours on the hill or in the village. This transition is hard for the child, as will be the birth of its small brother or sister.

The loss of the first milk-tooth shows that from now on the child can eat the same food as adults.

All these transitions are marked symbolically by rituals involving both the child and the parents.

The period which follows is marked by various rites of integration. Thus the first steps taken by the child are the occasion for family celebrations. The first words it speaks initiate a new style of communication. The child can then grow up with the different age-groups. With the different roles that it plays, the child learns to exercise leadership and organize creativity. Children train one another up through the age-groups, thus creating bonds for life. These groups are particularly important in societies where there is collective initiation at the age of puberty. This was the usual network for growing together in social, sexual and religious life.

During this period of growth, initiation into the mysteries of life takes place in a subtle, discreet and informal way. For girls, aunts play a greater role than the mother. The aunts explain the different physiological functions which come about with puberty and the different forms of behaviour to be adopted. They teach a girl how to run a house, how to treat men, how to live in a family which is not hers, and all that the girl will need for her future existence. These educational exchanges can take place between different age groups when the girls meet to fetch water, when they gather to collect wood or when they go on walks.

For boys, debates and chat in the public place became the schools of life. There, in addition to techniques of living, the young men learned to perpetuate tradition together in the land of their ancestors. Furthermore the boy had to keep close to his father to be initiated into conduct and discipline in life and to learn a job.

For both boys and girls this period from infancy to puberty was meant to make it possible to integrate into their lives the function and the significance of rites connected with 'being born', 'growing up', 'marriage', 'being sick', 'dying', 'the changing of the seasons', 'the history of the clan', the 'humour of the ancestors', 'social allies' and so on. The period was enough for them to achieve mastery of proverbs, stories, riddles, songs, lullabies, sayings, the whole literary ensemble which sums up the historical experience of a people.

In social groups connected with initiation to puberty, there had to be a period of intense training. This summed up the whole of life and irreversibly opened up a new adult existence.

The initiation of boys, for example, was singularly instructive.

The festivals, rites and tests which mark the passage to adulthood generally contain the following elements: segregation, retreat, communal life, separation from the mother and women in general, the *auto da fé* of all that recalls the old existence, instructions given by the elders, ritual nudity or grass garments recalling the first human beings, baths of purification, tests of bravery and courage, fasting, beating, ragging, various mutilations or scars, secret languages, new names, initiations into life, customs, the mysteries of society, exercises of physical and military training, songs, dances, the usage of the sacred instruments, masks, drums, etc.[3]

Throughout the educational process, collective responsibility and functioning by age-groups was constantly evident. The child was never the property only of the father and mother. The child was a common 'good' of the tribe, the clan, the village, the country. Anyone could look after it and bring help in case of need. It was even permissible to punish someone else's child if it was at fault and tell the parents afterwards.

After being trained in this way, the young man or woman could enter into marriage and adulthood. Nevertheless, social coming of age only took place with the birth of the first child.

Other rites of passage were organized to mark the menopause, death, mourning, the end of mourning, sharing an inheritance, settling family conflicts, and the decomposition of the body which led to the invisible world.

The invisible world remained very present, hence the building of a house for the ancestors in a corner of the family enclosure. There communion rites with the deceased grandparents took place, with food and libations of traditional drinks. Similarly, the family house had to be built with an opening at the top to allow the surveillance of the eye of the *Imana* God and the coming of the spirit of the ancestor in case of need. The true state of ancestor was reserved for those who had lived well as wise, heroic and model men. The good-for-nothings were condemned to see their spirit wandering endlessly and without repose.

3. Perpetuation of the vital force and participation in the invisible world

The perpetuation of the vital force was a duty for all. This was brought about by inserting the child into its cultural milieu; it had to master the different ways of wisdom in it. The child was also a project in the sense that it had to make its personal contribution to the growth of the life of the clan by realizing the prowess which attached to its particular genius. This could be in community work or in hunting, war, or social agreements and pacts.

Beyond the techniques called for by all this, the child, like the whole of society, developed in a universe which was symbolically unified as a constellation of vital elements related to the invisible. That explains why such importance was attached to ritual life. Life was marked out with sacrifices and divinations by the father of the family (*serugo*), by the guardians of the secrets of the clan or the royal court (*abanyamabanga*), by initiates in the art of divination and healing (*apabfumu*). It was not a matter mainly of unveiling knowledge but of establishing or restoring physical and mystico-social equilibrium in the face of a threat to a family or region. We can understand the limitations of the medicine imported from the West in the imagination of populations with such a holistic vision.

Both blessings and curses performed a highly significant function. Here there was an enhanced need to master language.

This mystical and religious environment was particularly present in the conception of the child. The infant is always impregnated by the invisible world. It is the link with the ancestors and the genies. This was particularly felt in the case of the birth of abnormal or unusual children like albinos, monsters, dwarves, stillborn, children with teeth at birth, and abortions. These were situations which showed a lack of equilibrium or a break in the relationship with the invisible world of the *Imana* God, ancestors or some genies. The cause had to be discovered or the tabu had to be restored to re-establish the cosmic harmony through rites of purification and reconciliation. The birth of twins was special to the degree that it was seen as bringing as many blessings as threats. The ritual of the purification of the mother was more complex in this case. The father and mother of twins became 'tabu' persons with special powers, making them vehicles of blessings or curses.

4. *Bringing the child into the world as an attestation of social coming of age*

A woman who died without having given birth to a child was buried in the embryo position with a burnt piece of wood to symbolize that the vital current was definitely extinct in her. An arrow could also be put in the region of her kidneys to signify that the vital force was killed in her. As for dead children, the mourning ceremonies for this kind of dead person were reduced to the minimum. Similarly, important rites consisting of giving milk to the survivors of the family (*kunywa amata*) and ending mourning (*kuva ku rupfu*) were omitted or reduced to their simplest expression.

The importance of this state of parenthood shone through even the conception of marriage. As in many African groups, marriage in the Africa of the Great Lakes is never a matter for two individuals. It is a progressive alliance between two wider families of which the two spouses are symbolic concentrations. Where Western tradition presents marriage as a point in time at which consent is exchanged between the couple in front of witnesses approved of by law, followed by 'consummation', the tradition here recognizes the consummation of a marriage with the birth of the first child. To that point the marriage was only being progressively realized. A break coming before the birth of the first child, for example, would make it necessary to return the dowry paid by the family of the boy, while that could not happen after the birth of the first child. After this birth, both the young man and the young woman entered into the adult category and acquired a certain family and social independence in their affairs. The woman then entered her husband's clan as an adult and could take part in the various deliberations.

Similarly, a young man or a bachelor was never invested with social responsibility as a notable of the hill, village and clan (*kwatira*). He had to be the father of a family in order to be responsible for social affairs, after having learned to look after his family affairs. The priestly ordination of the Catholic church into the social responsibilities which priesthood involves is an innovation in the culture of the Africa of the Great Lakes, as compared with the social coming of age conferred by the birth of the first child.

Being a father or mother is a true source of human flourishing, attesting that one has fulfilled the duty of handing on life, that one has become socially adult and will be able to leave one's trace in human history. Successful education of a child comes as something else to be proud of. Nothing was sought so much as an extended old age in the midst of a multitude of descendants with good social positions.

That, schematically, is the milieu of the traditional culture in which the child discovered life and the universe. By an integrative process it learnt the art and wisdom of life in a social and family framework with a functionalized pedagogy of roots and creation. The important thing was to establish harmonious relations with its universe.

II The child of today confronted with two epistemological heritages

The rise of the West in African milieux as a result of the movements of colonization and evangelization has seized the imagination of Africans in a very complex way. From now on their destiny is bound up with world trade.[4] Our encounter and our trade were inevitably fatal to us because of a lack of criticism of the metaphysical and social choices within our cultural traditions at the moment of the encounter.

1. The world as conflict – the world as harmony

We will already have sensed that from tender infancy the child in the region of the African Great Lakes was educated to create harmonious links with its environment, both visible and invisible. The knowledge which it acquired was to permit it to find its place in the universe. The child learned to know who and what to avoid and the necessary partners for alliances.

Rooted in a society the basis of which, essential to the spirit, is the vision of the world as harmony, we find ourselves confronted with a civilization which had other metaphysical choices, 'those of reality as conflict and life as mastery of the fundamental laws of things; those of clear knowledge as a capital value and the submission of the world to the creative spirit proper to the human person and his or her being; those of utopia as a field of the possible and a concrete demand for the transformation of all things according to the will of human beings'.[5]

In going to school our children still draw on the family heritage; but at the same time they find themselves confronted with this new epistemology coming from the West.

2. *The increasing aggressiveness of foreign audio-visual media*

The information and media war have become imperatives of survival for today's society. This is all the more important as the globalization of life leads to the refinement of strategies for the ever-increasing extension of zones of influence. This explains the rapid growth of the number of FM relay stations for the major Western broadcasting companies in many African villages and the satellite relays for television.

These powerful media, with very seductive marketing, work in an aggressive way on the subconscious. They induce 'new values', often regarded by traditional society as counter-values. They exert pressure towards the appropriation of new family and social models by inviting conformity to the dominant model. All this inevitably works towards the destructurizing of a society so that it corresponds to the paradigm which can serve the interests of the international world of capitalism. It becomes difficult for children and young people to resist these attractions. The dilemma of the situation is that these tele-visual models do not have an already-structured field of integration in the social conscience for bringing about discernment and reconstruction.

What school? For what society?

The context and objectives of education differ visibly between the perspective of traditional society and that which mobilizes modern society. Where there is a preoccupation today with the transmission of knowledge and techniques, traditional society found itself responsible for conveying a message from the other world which it had progressively to bring to a maturity that would allow the vital current to blossom, through various rites of passage and integration. To educate was to allow the vital force to come into the world, to reveal itself, to build society, to reinforce the power of the family and the clan.

The integration of the two visions of the school are in conflict today. Moreover this is made worse by the situation of modern life, above all in its growth towards an urbanization which brings about a new restructuring of families. The new imperatives of life in the new society inevitably lead to the phenomena of street children and prostitution. Orphans who formerly were looked after by the wider family are now left on the periphery of society. In the best cases they are rescued by orphanages, the conception of which is far from being culturally integrated. It is unfortunate in this context that the orphans of wars and AIDS are becoming increasingly numerous in this region.

In the new context the challenge remains that of allowing the two epistemologies to help each other to be mutually fruitful and to allow the emergence of new 'older initiators', not only for knowledge and techniques, but also for life and experiential wisdom.

Translated by John Bowden

Notes

1. Rwanda, Burundi, eastern Zaire, western Tanzania, southern Uganda.
2. Taken from P. Erny, *L'enfant dans la pensée traditionelle de l'Afrique noire*, Paris 1990, 144.
3. Ibid., 164.
4. Alvin Toffler, *Powershift, Knowledge, Wealth and Violence at the Edge of the Twenty-First Century*, New York 1990, is instructive here.
5. Kä Mana, *Foi Chrétienne, Crise africaine et reconstruction de l'Afrique. Sens et enjeux des théologies africaines contemporaines (CETA, HAHO, CLÉ)*, Lome 1992, 125.

Youth at Risk: The Covenant House Experience

Mary Rose McGeady

The call of the gospel for the care of our children seems to speak louder to us today than ever. This is not a good era for children. Throughout the world, we read continually of the suffering and abuse that children are undergoing. We have heard the horror stories of 40,000 orphans left from the wars in Rwanda, and like numbers from Somalia. In Latin America, in Brazil, Peru and Guatemala, we are aware of shootings of homeless 'street kids' simply for being on the street and begging.

With amazing speed, the world seems to forget these numbers, and within weeks after their publication on the front pages of newspapers and television screens everywhere, the world ceases even to comment on the reality of these hundreds of thousands of children. And, in the First World, children are suffering neglect and abuse of proportions never known before.

In the United States of America, which has long prided itself on making children a high priority and on encouraging research and creativity in the care of children, the situation is worsening every day. It was recently reported that nearly four million American children are growing up in neighbourhoods with high rates of poverty, absent fathers, unemployment and reliance on public welfare assistance. We can no longer be surprised by the terrible outcomes experienced by young people who grow up in environments where drugs, violence, welfare and teenage pregnancy are far more prevalent than safe schools, high school diplomas, happy homes and good jobs. Many neighbourhoods offer poor children no real choices.

One recent study[1] which sought to quantify the number of children in stressful neighbourhoods studied Census Bureau data and found that

nearly half of the 3.9 million children living in very troubled neighbourhoods were from six of the largest states of the USA: California,
Illinois, Michigan, New York, Ohio and Texas. Every state except one,
out of the fifty states, had such neighbourhoods. The study used five
indicators to determine if a neighbourhood was troubled: 1. a poverty rate
above 28%; 2. more than 40% of households headed by women; 3. a high
school drop-out rate – over 23%; 4. more than 47% of men 'unattached to
the labour force'; and 5. more than 17% of families on welfare. A
neighbourhood with four of the five indicators was labeled as 'severely
distressed'.

Other findings in this study included:

– One out of every four Black children lives in a severely depressed
neighbourhood, compared with one of every 10 Hispanic children and
one of every 63 White children;
– One quarter of all children under six live in poverty and over half of
them in a family headed by a woman;
– Births to single teenagers are increasing in all but three American
states;
– The violent death rate for teenagers rose 13% between 1985 and 1991.
While death of fifteen- to nineteen-year-olds caused by accidents
decreased by 15%, death by homicide doubled.
– The violent crime arrest rate for youths aged ten to seventeen
increased 50% between 1985 and 1991. In 1985 it was 305 per 100,000
youth; in 1991 it rose to 457 per 100,000.

What the statistics do is document the reality that we see lived out among
us, and that reality can be defined as an increasing neglect of our youth. In
an era when it is increasingly difficult to grow up in healthy surroundings,
we find that societal supports for a positive framework are giving way on
too many fronts.

Let me speak first of the family. We see in the United States a very
serious – a very gradual, but real – deterioration of the family structure. We
now acknowledge a divorce rate of 50% for first marriages and 70% for
second marriages. The reality is that many children are caught up in this
failure, and adolescents especially are involved in the dissolution of many
second marriages. Over and over, in our work at Covenant House, we hear
the story of an adolescent who tells us that his parents were divorced when
he was five, but within two years both of his parents re-married. For the
rest of his growing-up years he was passed from one parent to the other,
lacking a sense of belonging and a sense of stability. Such young people

frequently make statements like, 'I never felt that I belonged in either place and I never really got over the loss of my own father. And, I never really felt close to my stepfather.'

In families where divorce has not been a factor, the reality of having two working parents has weakened the relational bonding between parent and child. It is now common in the United States for a mother to return to work within three weeks of the birth of a new child, and the care of her newborn is thus relegated to another for the remainder of its childhood, with the time with the parent markedly reduced. The long-term effect of this lack of parental time during the early years is, without a doubt, one of the factors that is contributing to the enormous turmoil in the lives of adolescents. Rates of disturbance have skyrocketed and increase every year.

An alarming number of adolescents are in crisis, have left home and are indeed 'disconnected kids'. From my perspective the situation is truly an American tragedy.

The 'disconnected kids', the product of the enormous paradigm-shifts in culture, in family structures and values, are kids who have lost that most critical of social necessities: a sense of belonging. The most vital element of human connectedness, the parent/child relationship, is disrupted, and the adolescent experiences the pain and discomfort of feeling totally alone, suspended in space, without roots, without a base to cling to – in a word, disconnected. At a time when all the usual pressures of adolescence impinge, the youngster loses the very groundedness that offered some perspective: family. Although most adolescents decry the vital role these parental relationships play in their lives, their behaviours proclaim their enormous need for the balance these relationships provide.

Sad to say, the trauma in the lives of so many parents who have lived through the horrors of abandonment, rejection, divorce or separation is frequently so damaging that in the midst of such struggles parents lose, at least temporarily, the capacity to be a stabilizing and balancing factor in the lives of their own children. Many parents undergo role reversal and begin to rely on their children to meet their needs. More frequently, they are simply not adept as parents for long periods of time. The result is often conscious or unconscious rejection of their adolescent child, especially if the latter is showing signs of adjustment or relational problems. The task is just too great for the parent. The result is too much for the adolescent. The outcome – disconnectedness! The relationship sours, open conflict becomes common, angry words become the standard mode of communication, and physical abuse often begins. It is also not uncommon for hurting parents to seek sexual satisfaction by abusing children or adolescents in incestuous relationships.

Reconstituted or blended families created by remarriage following divorce also frequently suffer from the inability of an adolescent child of one spouse to adjust and relate to the new parent. Unresolved feelings, pro or con, on the part of the adolescent for the lost parent, and expectations on the part of the new parent frequently lead to the same feelings of rejection, anger and open conflict previously experienced by the adolescent. Often, instead of the hurt of divorce being healed by remarriage, these pains are indeed deepened, and the adolescent feels even further removed from the original parent – even further disconnected.

Once one is in touch with the potency and depth of this disconnectedness, one has a greater empathy for the action so common to many adolescents – to run away from it all.

These distressing factors are also contributing to the fact that there are increasing numbers of 'street kids' in our major cities all over the world. These are kids who have run away from unhappy home situations, usually characterized by the factors that are mentioned above, or kids who have been thrown out by parents who cannot adequately cope with the troubled behaviours so often exhibited by these kids.

Covenant House International is a programme targeting the care of 'street kids'. In addition to programmes in nine American cities, Covenant House sponsors programmes in Canada, Mexico, Guatemala and Honduras. Everywhere we see increasing numbers of street kids who lack the support and love of a caring family. Some of these young people have been on the street for fairly short periods of time, ranging from a few days to a few weeks. Others have lived on the street for considerably longer, and occasionally we meet adolescents who have been there for as long as three years. They learn to live by their wits, they become 'street smart', and many turn to drug selling or to prostitution for a steady income. Others with less experience are terrified by the harsh realities of street life. Because of the AIDS epidemic, hustlers recruit younger and younger teenagers to participate in prostitution. We encounter thirteen-year-olds who are experienced prostitutes.

We state our mission as follows:

We who recognize God's providence and fidelity to his people are dedicated to living out his covenant among ourselves and those children we serve, with absolute respect and unconditional love. That commitment calls us to serve suffering children of the street, and to protect and safeguard all children. Just as Christ in his humanity is the visible sign of God's presence among his people, so our efforts together in the covenant community are a visible sign that effects the presence of God, working through the Holy Spirit among ourselves and our kids.

In the living out of our mission, we have certain key elements of approach:
1. *Outreach*. At all our Covenant Houses, we have staff whose specific responsibility is outreach on the streets. They go out, usually at night, either in vans or on foot, looking for kids who are living on the streets. Our attempt is to encounter and engage these youngsters, to develop an understanding of what has led them to this manner of life, and invite them into one of our shelters, to begin the process of rehabilitation. In many instances, the trust level of these adolescents has been so destroyed by the adults that have been key figures in their lives that it is difficult to have them again trust adults who are reaching out to them. Sometimes we have to meet these young people many times on the street, as part of our outreach effort, before they are ready to trust us and accept our interventions. Many of them reach a point of readiness and come, on their own, into our crisis shelters.
2. *Crisis Centres*. We attempt to be as accepting and welcoming as possible, and our 'Open Intake' policy means that we do not wait for formal referrals or official papers of any kind, but accept any youngster who comes to our door, asking to be admitted. They are, of course, free to leave at any time and some do leave within a day or two. But with those who are willing to stay longer, we have an opportunity to begin the restoration of hope and a brighter future. The average stay in our crisis shelters is about three weeks. For those who do need longer rehabilitation time, we offer a programme that we call the Rights of Passage programme, in which youngsters can stay up to two years. In order to be a resident in this programme, they must be working, going to school and, in many instances, undertaking job training for more reliable employment.

While the youngster is in the crisis shelter, we make great efforts to determine whether a return to home and family is a possibility. Sad to say, we find every year that fewer and fewer adolescents are able to return home because the family situation is so characterized by alcoholism, drug addiction or generalized conflict that it is not only not a desirable situation, but in many instances a disastrous one. We find that increasing numbers of the young people who come to us are coming out of foster care. Many have been in foster care situations where they were very unhappy, and youngsters have even recounted being placed as many as seventeen times in different foster homes or group homes, so that they are totally disillusioned with the child welfare system which has not provided home and happiness for them.

3. *Counselling.* A key element in our work with every adolescent who comes to us is the counselling relationship, which is essentially a supportive, affirming one, critically geared toward restoring to these youngsters a self-concept characterized by positive assessments of their chances of 'making it' in the future. We hear a lot of depression; we hear a lot of discouragement; we hear a lot of negative feelings about themselves from these youngsters who have had little or no affirmation and encouragement in their lives. Many tell us that they are 'bad' children and have been the cause of their family problems. Our counselling work is very much a reversal of this negative self-concept, which is so destructive to their learning processes as well as their hope. But, thank God, we see a lot of resurrections out of the death-dealing experiences that they have lived with over many years. We find seeds of resiliency, which we labour assiduously to grow. We fan the flames of self-confidence as we see it begin to emerge, fragile though it be. We truly believe that 'nothing succeeds like success', and we try to provide small instances of success which begin the cycle of affirmation and resiliency.

4. *Rights of Passage.* For those youngsters for whom the best plan is independence with a job and a place to live, we have a programme which we call Rights of Passage and which is based on the philosophy that we believe a young person has the right to be accompanied on the passage to adulthood. In order to come into the Rights of Passage programme a young person must have demonstrated his or her seriousness of purpose, and the resolution to turn their lives around and to carry through on their plan for rehabilitation. The key to this process is holding a job. In some instances this is full-time and in others part-time, but the world of work in this process is of paramount importance, because the reality is that the greatest hope of most of these young people is for a job that will allow them to earn sufficient money to support themselves and live independently. This part of the programme indeed completes the cycle which started with the removal of the young person from street life, the offering of a second chance, and the development of a plan through its realization. We have seen hundreds of adolescents enter and succeed in this programme, and they have demonstrated to us that, in most instances, when young people are given opportunities to suceed, with the necessary affirmation and support, they are more than anxious to make use of such opportunities.

Throughout our process there is no more important element than the care and love which we try to offer to every young person. Gradually, as their hostilities and resistances dissipate, they are able to believe that we truly care and they are much more willing to accept the help that is offered.

5. *Pastoral care*. Pastorally, we make a significant effort to reach these young people on a faith level. For the most part they have been 'unchurched', and have very little religious instruction or religious experience, and we are indeed challenged to offer them the image of a loving, caring God when so much of their lives have not been characterized by such experiences. While we do not proselytize, we try to instil in the youngsters the conviction that there is a God who created and died for them and to whom they can pray. One of the most successful efforts of our pastoral experiences has been the daily morning prayer sessions where the young people come to the chapel and read from a portion of Scripture which they choose, and then stand in a circle with their arms on each other's shoulders and pray spontaneously. In those instances where we have children who are identifiably Catholic, we do arrange for sacramental preparation.

What to Do

The Scriptures have spoken to us poignantly about our responsibility. Isaiah admonishes us: 'Learn to do right. See that justice is done . . . help those who are oppressed, give orphans their rights, and defend widows' (Isa. 1. 17). The words of Jesus are never more powerful than in Matthew 25, where he identifies himself with the 'least of our brothers and sisters'. I think that disconnected kids fit these scriptural descriptions.

Little by little, over the last thirty years, each segment of society has decreased its investment in our youth. In the days of my youth, rare was the parish without a youth programme – usually a combination of religious, social and athletic events – and usually, too, under the direction of its youngest priest. Now, fewer and fewer parishes sponsor such programmes, often under the pressure of staggering insurance premiums that accompany undertakings like teen-age dances or sports programmes. Youth programmes, i.e., boys and girls clubs, and youth centres, are a disappearing breed. Kids now turn to shopping malls and 'bright light zones' as the places to 'be', and the values available to them there breed neither religious nor civic virtues.

The Catholic Church has long been a bell-ringer on social systems that are not working, and it needs now to ring the bell hard to awaken our society to the fact that the numbers of throwaway children and its disconnected kids are growing at a frightening pace. A society that can so waste its youth is indeed frittering away its future, and the longer we wait to pay the bill, the higher the toll.

The church needs to make support for family life a priority on its advocacy agenda and on its own internal service agenda as well.

In my opinion, more than anything else, parishes and agencies need to initiate parenting assistance programmes that help parents to cope *before* crisis hits. Many youth problems could be confronted more effectively if parents were forearmed by quality programmes in parenting that would help them to anticipate and cope more competently.

In the best of all worlds, or at least in a better world, local school and parish-based classes for all parents would be available – taught by experienced parents with professional consultation on hand. This kind of support to families, accompanied by youth programmes, would also strengthen the links among parishioners and promote genuine community, a reality so hard to achieve in the modern American parish.

The actions needed truly to address the problems discussed here are multiple. They must be both swift and short-term and structured and long-term. In the short run, the kids need care – a continuum of awareness and commitment to action which will keep building programmes of response – outreach, shelter, loving rehabilitation, training for employment, aftercare and new opportunities for independent living. Covenant House is one attempt at such a continuum of care. But more is needed. There has to be a raising of consciousness among our people about the thousands of adolescents who are in crisis so that more adequate responses will be forthcoming.

Notes

1. *Kids Count Data Book: State Profiles of Child Well Being*, Annie E. Casey Foundation 1995.

How the Family Became a 'Liberal Issue' in the United States

Don Browning

For years, in the political culture of the United States, the family was seen as a conservative issue. Both Republicans Ronald Reagan and George Bush were elected to the presidency by championing the rhetoric of family values. They successfully appealed to political conservatives, Christian evangelicals, fundamentalists and conservative Catholics. Their family rhetoric helped them capture the highest office of the land.

In 1992 this strategy failed. Vice-presidential candidate Dan Quayle, in his famous Murphy Brown address, attempted to implement it once again. Murphy Brown, a sitcom television news woman played by actress Candice Bergen, decided to have a baby out of wedlock. Dan Quayle attacked the Murphy Brown show, and the television and movie industry in general, for undermining family values and undercutting the importance of the two-parent family. This time the Republican appeal to family values backfired. Bill Clinton and Al Gore successfully depicted the family values rhetoric as a ploy to avoid serious issues pertaining to the economy, health care and welfare reform. Bush and Quayle lost the election, and for a brief time it seemed that the family issue would vanish from the US political, cultural and religious agenda.

This impression soon proved to be wrong. What really happened was that the family issue became a liberal issue. It might be more accurate to say it became a neo-liberal issue. For the last two years, the political culture of the United States has undergone a significant realignment, and the family issue is at the core of a new set of conversations and a new set of alliances. Why has this happened?

Family as a conservative issue

The family was thought to be a conservative issue in the 1970s and 1980s for a wide range of reasons. First, the family in both church and political culture began to be seen as a privatistic issue. The victory of the civil rights movement set the stage for both the religious and political culture. Institutional racial discrimination was ended through Supreme Court rulings, legislative enactments and state enforcement of the law. It did not come about by converting individuals one at a time. For this reason, it suddenly seemed logical to effect social change of all kinds from the top down – at the level of large-scale change in social systems rather than at the level of individuals and families. This emphasis on large-scale social change also corresponded with Marxism and its stress on class revolution and radical alterations in the means of production. One can find a similar emphasis in liberation theology, which has, in fact, had a decided impact on the leadership of the liberal American churches. For a decade before the Republican party picked up 'family values' as a campaign theme, the leadership of liberal religion and liberal politics believed that family problems were primarily social systemic problems – the result of discrimination, inadequate distribution of wealth, and lack of access to the educational and occupational goods of society. If family problems existed (and many doubted that they did), then governmental policies, welfare and universal education would gradually eradicate them. From one perspective, the conservative emphasis on the 'values' that held families together was an antithesis to a prior liberal thesis. This liberal thesis was that social conditions, not individual or family values, were the important variables affecting the health of families and their children.

The neo-liberal, neo-conservative conversation

There is more to this story that could be told. But this should be sufficient to illustrate how the conversation has changed. The sociologist James Davison Hunter in his 1990 book called *Culture Wars* classified the parties in the family debate as orthodox or conservatives and liberals or progressives. From 1992 to the November elections of 1994, a conversation developed between an emerging group of mediating political, cultural and religious leaders. It occurred between a new group of 'neo-liberals' and a new group of 'neo-conservatives'. Neo-liberals at that time were liberals who still believed that government intervention in the areas of families, education and welfare was necessary for overcoming poverty, discrimination and injustice. These same neo-liberals were also beginning to believe that cultural values are important – that the values people hold about family formation, family preservation, and the importance of children are crucial to the common good. Neo-liberals included the Democratic Leadership Council, the Communitarian Movement (led by Amitai Etzioni, Mary Ann Glendon and Jean Bethke Elshtain), the leadership of the Institute for American Values, William Galston (at that time Deputy Domestic Adviser to President Clinton) and Clinton himself. At that time it was, and still is, difficult to find mainline churches which articulated explicitly neo-liberal public policy views.

It was difficult sometimes to distinguish neo-liberals from neo-conservatives on the family issue during that period. On the whole, however, neo-conservatives were more likely to emphasize deteriorating cultural values in their diagnosis of family troubles. They were also more sceptical of government solutions than neo-liberals. But this was precisely where the change had come about. There emerged a group of formerly conservative individuals and institutions that began proposing a variety of governmental supports for families – some of which were quite expensive.

The conservative Family Research Council – at one time, but no longer, the policy wing of Christian psychologist James Dobson's *Focus on the Family* – is a good example. This conservative think-tank has proposed a number of tax measures to support families with children, encourage family formation and support poor two-parent families. It has been less interested in direct welfare payments and more interested in tax measures for families that encourage welfare independence and employment. At the same time that some neo-conservatives began to contemplate new forms of government support other than direct welfare payments, many neo-liberals were themselves beginning to lose faith in traditional welfare programmes. In short, a new convergence between neo-liberals and neo-conservatives began to emerge, with neo-liberals taking cultural values more seriously and neo-conservatives taking more seriously the need for government involvement in families.

This fragile consensus contained one genuinely surprising element: both neo-liberals and neo-conservatives began to hold that government needs to go beyond moral neutrality on family issues and state a public ethic for families. The political talk of both neo-liberals, such as Clinton and Galston, and neo-conservatives, such as the Family Research Council, exhibited a new moral language about the importance of the intact two-parent family, the importance of putting children first, the importance of fathers for families, the importance of paternal accountability, and the moral and practical need to discourage teen-age pregnancies and out-of-wedlock births. Americans also heard both groups struggle to re-envision more creative, less dependency-producing government assistance to all kinds of families where the welfare of children was involved. Of course, since the Republican victories of late 1994, this fragile alliance of neo-liberals and neo-conservatives has been swamped, at least for the moment, by more conservative forces. In the long run, however, the creative convergence may reassert itself and lead the way to a more viable solution to the family crisis facing American society.

Why liberals became interested in the values issue

Why did some political liberals suddenly become interested in family formation, family preservation, the renewal of marriage and the moderation of divorce? The answer is at least two-fold: 1. the growing evidence documenting the deteriorating health and economic condition of children and single mothers; and 2. the growing violence among children of broken families and single parents.

Evidence for the growing poverty of single mothers and the deteriorating mental and physical health of children is the weightiest factor influencing this change of mind. Increased divorce and out-of-wedlock births are now being seen as the proximate causes behind these trends. Take divorce. The 1970s and 1980s saw a tremendous rise in the divorce rate in the US; it now stands at around 50% and is predicted to go higher. It was not until the mid-1980s, with the research of Lenore Weitzman and Greg Duncan, that Americans began to understand that divorce corresponded to a precipitous decline in the economic well-being of mothers and their children – about a 30% drop during the first year after divorce in contrast to a 15% increase for divorcing men. According to one study, about 10% of white children and 14% of black children whose parents separated fell into poverty the following year.

If one combines the consequences of divorce with those of out-of-wedlock births, the facts look darker. Forty-five per cent of female-headed families with children under eighteen are poor in contrast to only 7% of families with children headed by a married couple. In the US, fathers of divorce do not, on the whole, support their children very well, either financially or emotionally. Child-support payments amount to only 10% of the income of separated and single mothers and 13% of the income of divorced mothers. In addition, divorced fathers spend little time with their children. According to one national study conducted in 1981, only one

child in six saw his or her father as often as once a week, and close to half
had not visited with their fathers in the twelve months preceding the study.

Declining economic well-being, declining attention from fathers, and
mounting stress on poor and overworked mothers – all of these factors have
resulted in deteriorating mental and physical health of children in the US.
A 1988 national survey conducted by the Department of Health and
Human Services showed that 20% of children between three and seventeen
had a developmental, learning or behavioural disorder. By the time they
reached the age of twelve to seventeen, one in four had one of these
difficulties; among boys, the rate was one in three. The report identified
the decline of the stable two-parent family as a major factor behind these
trends. Other indices of child well-being are equally discouraging. The
economists Victor Fuchs and Diane Reklis report that between 1960 and
1980 teenage suicide rates tripled, standardized academic test scores fell,
obesity rates (and associated symptoms of hypertension, psycho-social
problems, respiratory disease and diabetes) also climbed during this
period. The correlation between teenage crime and broken homes became
clearer. Louis Sullivan, former secretary of the US Department of Health
and Human Services, reported that over 70% of young males in prison
come from homes where the father was absent.

The great shift in the liberal consensus

These facts began to weigh on the conscience of almost everyone interested
in the national good. They also weighed on the consciences of many
liberals deeply committed to social justice. What did they mean? Were they
true? Were they the result of a changing, indeed corrupt, new set of
individualistic and self-indulgent values? Or were they due to changing
economic conditions and unjust social practices? Or were both sets of
factors involved?

Declining economic conditions and inadequate governmental programmes are clearly a factor, but there is new information suggesting that their
importance can be exaggerated. Changing values and declining commitment to marriage, family and children explain more than liberals once
thought. For instance, the economists Fuchs and Reklis in a 1992 article
published in the prestigious *Science* magazine demonstrate how the
decline in the physical and emotional well-being of children began in the
US in the 1970s when there was less child poverty, higher family incomes
and more government investment in children than ever before. Fuchs and
Reklis conclude:

Both cultural and material changes have probably contributed to the problems of America's children; the relative importance of the different explanations, however, varies over time. Between 1960 and 1970 the fall in test scores, the doubling of teenage suicide and homicide rates, the doubling share of birth to unwed mothers cannot be attributed to economic adversity. During that decade purchases of goods and services for children by government rose very rapidly, as did real household income per child, and the poverty rate of children plummeted. Thus, we must seek explanations for the rising problems of that period in the cultural realm.[1]

In the decade of the 1980s, Fuchs and Reklis point out that economic conditions in the US for families and children did grow worse. But their interpretation goes something like this: declining economic conditions further aggravated deteriorations in childhood emotional and physical health – deteriorations caused first by the cultural shifts of the preceding decade of the 1970s. By shifts in the cultural realm, they mean increased individualism, careerism and the growing tendency to resolve conflicts of interests between adults and children in favour of the interests of adults.

One measure of this cultural shift was the lower amount of time that adults spent with children. During the 1970s the birth rate fell. The result was that there were more adults to take care of fewer children. There should have been more time available for children. But a 1985 study by a University of Maryland sociologist reported that parents spend seventeen hours a week with their children in contrast to thirty hours in 1965. A very recent report shows that it is the middle- and upper-middle class suburbanites, in contrast to the inner-city poor, who are more likely to leave their children alone and unsupervised. A recent Census Bureau report states, 'children most likely to be left unsupervised lived in suburbs, where the rate was 9.3%, as opposed to 6.8% in cities and 5.3% in rural areas'. One news account reports that 'high-income individuals and those with some college education were more likely than others to leave children unattended'. Thus, the declining amount of time spent with children is not a matter of economic necessity alone.

The economic explanation of family decline has been further qualified by the work of my University of Chicago colleagues Mark Testa and William Julius Wilson. Wilson's 1987 book entitled *The Truly Disadvantaged* advanced the thesis that the problems of poor, inner-city families were due to the flight of industry and jobs from the inner city.[2] Inner-city men, most of whom were black, could not form families because they could not afford to support them – hence the explosion of out-of-wedlock births and absent fathers. There is no question that Wilson's thesis is largely true, but it is now being revised. His colleague Mark Testa found that the values of inner-city black males have changed since the 1940s, reflecting changes in the wider society. Even when black males do get jobs and move into the middle classes, they are more reluctant to marry, even the women that give birth to their children.[3] Wilson's next book is expected to emphasize the importance of both cultural values and economic conditions, and will begin to explore the importance of culture-making institutions, such as inner-city churches, in reconstructing the value commitments of black men. No one can visit the black churches surrounding the University of Chicago where I teach without learning that it is precisely this agenda to reconstitute the black family by reordering the values of black males that is central to these churches.[4]

The growing recognition of the importance of family stability and family form was reflected in a recent address given by the moral philosopher and policy analyst William Galston, formerly Deputy Assistant on Domestic Affairs to President Clinton. Family structure, he argues, affects the well-being of children more than race. His favourite statistic comes from the *Kids Count* report of the Casey Foundation. The children of single-parent teenagers were ten times more likely to be in poverty than the children of young married couples who finished high school and waited to the age of twenty to have their first child. Furthermore, Galston reports Census Bureau statistics to the effect that 'the children of white single-parent families are two-and-a-half times more likely to be living in poverty than are the children in black two-parent families'.[5]

Such reports explain why Charles Murray's October 1993 editorial in the *Wall Street Journal* received such a positive hearing, even among neo-liberals who did not agree with everything that he says.[6] Murray, a fellow at the American Enterprise Institute and author of the 1984 *Losing Ground*,[7] argued in that editorial that the trend toward out-of-wedlock births, now at 68% in the US black community, is spreading to the white community and promises to create a new white underclass. The out-of-wedlock birth rate in the white community is now at 22%, the rate that existed in the black community in the early 1960s when the rate in the white community was only 5%. Murray argued that social attitudes toward family formation and out-of-wedlock births are changing rapidly and are far more permissive than they once were, even among working and middle-class whites. As a result of these value changes, there now exists the possibility of an explosion of out-of-wedlock births in the white community, with a potential drastic downward spiral in the standard of living by single-parent families that get trapped in this spreading trend. Murray, as is well known, would correct this trend to taking all government support or welfare away from mothers giving birth out of wedlock. This is a radical cure which might not cure at all. What is new, however, in the US is that many liberals, deeply concerned with social justice and the needs of poor women and children, are now willing to take Murray's diagnosis more seriously, even though they reject his solutions.

These recognitions have led much of American liberal political culture to reject the thinking advanced by sociologists such as Jesse Barnard or the 1977 Carnegie report which claimed that diversity of family form was a benign inevitability and that the effect of family break-up need not be serious. It is not surprising that in the 1991 report of the bi-partisan National Commission on Children chaired by Senator John Rockefeller, the following words were written:

> Children do best when they have the personal involvement and material support of a father and a mother and when both parents fulfil their responsibility to be loving providers . . . Rising rates of divorce, out-of-wedlock childbearing and absent parents are not just manifesta-tions of alternative lifestyles, they are patterns of adult behaviour that increase children's risk of negative consequences.[8]

Similar conclusions stated in even stronger terms were reached by a more recent report submitted to President Bush entitled *Families First*. The report argues that: 'The trend of family fragmentation drives the nation's most pressing social problems: crime, educational failure, declining mental health, drug abuse, and poverty. These in turn further fragment families.'[9]

The role of religion in the US family debate

Where are American religious institutions in this new interest in the moral and value dimension of the family discussion? The answer goes something like this. Most mainline Protestant denominations are split between conservative and progressive wings. The bureaucratic leadership of these denominations tends to consist of old-style liberals who are, for the most part, slow to understand the present dimensions of the family crisis in the US. When they do address family issues, they are likely to combine a message of social justice with an economic analysis of the reasons for the declining well-being of children and mothers. These denominations have little to say about how churches can help in reconstructing the values supporting a post-industrial, egalitarian, mother-father team dedicated to the flourishing of children. Much of the leadership of the mainstream Protestant denominations assumes the analysis of the older liberalism and seems not to have taken the turn represented in the new conversations between neo-liberals and neo-conservatives in the arena of political culture.

Protestant evangelicals, along with Protestant fundamentalists, have always seen family problems in terms of declining values. This is moderating somewhat as both religious and political neo-conservatives struggle to find new forms of governmental and economic supports for families. The Catholic Church in the US is very much in the middle. When it looks at family issues from the perspective of the task of the worshipping and confessing church, it is concerned to implement among the faithful the family ethics of the Catholic Church. The Catholic Church resists the entrance of the state into matters of birth control and sex education, but it generally supports a liberal to neo-liberal agenda on welfare supports and tax breaks for families.

A remarkable twist in contemporary alliances can be found in the fact that, when neo-liberals at the political level look for religious allies, they are more likely to turn to Evangelicals and Catholics than they are to liberal Protestants. This is because, most of all, the new neo-liberals want the church to be the church. What do I mean? They want religious bodies to be a place where a powerful family ethic – and its supporting narratives, rituals, and institutional patterns – is proclaimed and implemented in the religious socialization of their members. This could be seen in the December 1993 speech by Galston on the emerging family policy of the Clinton administration. After summarizing a vast array of economic and welfare initiatives of the Clinton administration to help families, he added that government 'must do this work in cooperation with perhaps the most important institutions in American civil society: namely, religious institutions. We cannot pretend that government can get the job done . . .unless we learn how to cooperate more fully and more effectively with religious institutions.'[10] Galston characterized this new governmental alliance with religious institutions in helping families as 'maximum feasible accommodation' between church and state.

Galston is a distinguished moral philosopher who was at that time on leave to the White House from the University of Maryland. In his 1991 book titled *Liberal Purposes*, he outlines with great force the role of religion in creating the cultural and moral prerequisites for a just and democratic state.'' Galston develops a theory of Aristotelian democracy in contrast to the model of juridical liberalism dominating ideas of democracy in recent liberal theory. Galston's Aristotelian democracy assumes that citizens must have a high degree of moral virtue and character. His Aristotelian theory of democracy envisions a democracy with quality, culture, taste and tradition. It is not a minimal juridical democracy that works only to implement a rigorously conceived minimal standard of justice with no concern to maximize standards of character, virtue and democratic citizenship. Galston believes that a just democracy requires virtuous citizens. Virtuous citizens will be by definition committed to family responsibilities and the care of children. In turn, strong families are required for the education of virtuous citizens. And finally, Galston believes religion is essential for the creation of the ethics, motivations and powerful socializing institutions required to form strong families and virtuous citizens. Galston, and other neo-liberals, want churches to be interested in productive and just government programmes for families. But they also want churches to clarify and implement their own ethical vision of families. This is the unique contribution of churches to the total economy of the common good.

Christianity and the family

Recent research on the development of the family in the West is suggesting that Christianity had a powerful and largely efficacious role. Churches made a crucial contribution to the development of strong families in the West. They have an important role to play in the future. Although Christianity was implicated in the patriarchal institutions of the Graeco-Roman world of antiquity, it exerted a discernible transformative influence on the status of women and the well-being of children. In this way, early Christianity laid foundations for the emergence of the companionate family so important for democratic, post-industrial societies. The Harvard biblical scholar Elizabeth Schüssler Fiorenza has shown how the pre-Pauline church developed a new discipleship of equals between males and females quite different from the male-female relations dominated by the honour-shame codes of Roman Hellenism.'² The Ephesians 5 passage which identifies the husband's relation to his family with Christ's sacrificial relation to the church is now being seen as having fractured the emphasis on male domination, the ethic of the double standard and the consignment of women to private space characteristic of the Graeco-Roman family. The early Christian house church, with its heightened role for female equality and leadership, became the model for the Christian household, literally shaping the family into the more egalitarian patterns of the early Christian ecclesia.[13]

Jack Goody in his *Development of Family and Marriage in Europe* (1983) argues that wherever Christianity spread, the oriental family structure with its powerful male-headed clans and lineages that served as governments as well as kinship systems seems to have declined.[14] Robert Shaffern argues that the emphasis on monogamy found in both early Christianity and Roman law transformed the family patterns of Germany and Ireland, where a variety of family patterns existed.[15] One of the most popular family patterns in pre-Christian Irish and German territories was polygyny. Polygyny attracted women into the wealthier households and left wandering bands of brigands, somewhat like the male gangs of modern cities, to live in forests, destroy and steal property, and abduct and rape women. Historian David Herlihy argues that wherever Christian morality spread, buttressed with remnants of Roman family law, the monogamous family grew, poor men found wives, and fathers began taking responsibility for their children.[16] Catholic canon law was the great systematizer of these trends and, with its strong emphasis on mutual consent between husband and wife as a condition for valid marriage, may have set the stage, as James Q. Wilson argues, for the rise of the concept of universal civil rights, a concept so important for the theories of modern liberal societies.[17]

Thomas Aquinas may have worked out the strongest theoretical rationales for the emerging family theory of the West. With remarkable consistency with modern theories of evolutionary biology, Aquinas saw marriage and the family as meeting the needs of highly dependent human infants for stable parental care by incorporating males into the nurture of their children. He was aware that human males were nearly unique among mammals in their practice of male involvement with the raising of their children. He also built a strong case for what fathers contribute to their children. Even though Aquinas recognized that polygyny provided the possibility of paternal investment in children, he rejected it as a servile institution for women that made it impossible for marriage to become genuine friendship between husband and wife.[18] When seen in context, Aquinas's sacramental view of marriage must be viewed as an argument for the necessity of male lifelong commitment to their families, especially thkir children. Aquinas himself presented this emphasis as a kind of antidote to the archaic mammalian male tendency, which contemporary human ecologists are now describing in detail, to procreate but not become involved with their children.[19] Catholic marital theory must be seen as an intricate and multi-layered effort to domesticate and restructure this archaic male reproductive strategy.

Some historians have even gone so far as to say that the emphasis on the intact, companionate family that Christianity helped establish in Western Europe m y have contributed to the emergence of capitalism and modernity.[20] This family form, it s thou ht, developed the intense socializing procedures (based on deep affections between children and their parents) required to produce disciplined, hardworking, rational capitalists and democratic citizens. We neednhot determine the truth of this provocative claim in order to entertain a more modest one – that Christianity contributed significantly to the developmnt of the companionate family and that this family has had a productive fit with liberal demoratic and liberal economic institutions. For these reasons, Christians should be alert to their continuing responsibilities to study and debbate the ethics of families and the values guiding their formation and pgeservation.

In the great debate over the future of families now sweeping over most Western democracies, the churches must put their eggs in two baskets. That is to say, they must have two equally balanced strategies – one pertaining to the values that should govern family life and another pertaining to just social and economic policies supporting families in their task of raising children. But there is no possibility of the churches finding their way on issues of social policy without being clear about their theory of family ethics. And for this, they must critically understand their heritage and what they have contributed to the formation of families in the past.

Notes

1. Victor Fuchs and Diane Reklis, 'America's Children: Economic Perspectives and Policy Options', *Science* 255, January 1992, 45.

2. William J. Wilson, *The Truly Disadvantaged: The Inner City, the Underclass and Public Policy*, Chicago 1987.

3. Mark Testa, 'Male Joblessness, Nonmarital Parenthood, and Marriage', a paper prepared for the Chicago Urban Poverty and Family Life Conference, September 1991.

4. For a description of the family ministry of a large black Pentecostal church on the south side of Chicago, see Don Browning, *A Fundamental Practical Theology* Minneapolis 1991, 278–91.

5. William Galston, 'Beyond the Murphy Brown Debate: Ideas for Family Policy', Institute for American Values Family Policy Symposium, New York City, 10 December 1993, 4.

6. Charles Murray, 'The Coming White Underclass', *Wall Street Journal*, 29 October 1993.

7. Charles Murray, *Losing Ground: American Social Policy 1950–1980*, New York 1984.

8. *Beyond Rhetoric: A New American Agenda for Children and Families*, Washington, DC 1991, xix.

9. *Families First: Report of the National Commission on America's Urban Families*, Washington, DC 1993, 9.

10. William Galston, 'Beyond the Murphy Brown Debate', 14.

11. William Galston, *Liberal Purposes*, Cambridge 1990.

12. Elizabeth Schüssler-Fiorenza, *In Memory of Her*, New York and London 1983, 140–54.

13. Stephen Barton, 'Paul's Sense of Place: An Anthropological Approach to Community Formation in Corinth', *New Testament Studies* 23, 1986, 74.

14. Jack Goody, *Development of Family and Marriage in Europe*, Cambridge 1983.

15. Robert Shaffern, 'Christianity and the Rise of the Nuclear Family', *America*, 7 May 1994, 13–15.

16. David Herlihy, *Medieval Households*, Cambridge, Mass. 1985.

17. James Q. Wilson, *The Moral Sense*, New York 1993, 204–5.

18. Thomas Aquinas, *Summa Contra Gentiles*, III, ii.

19. Ibid.

20. Peter Laslett, *Family Life and Illicit Love in Earlier Generations*, Cambridge 1977.

II · Analyses and Reflections

Children as Subjects[1]

Anton A. Bucher

One of the most fascinating scenes in human life is watching a child learning to walk. It pulls itself up by a table, looks at the sofa nearby and ventures a first step, balancing with its hands. A second step succeeds, and a third. But then its knee gives way, the child puts out its hand to protect itself, and falls flat on its stomach. However, it scrabbles around on all fours, gets up again, takes a few more steps – and then falls again. So it goes on, time and again, until it finally reaches the toy in the far corner of the room.

If we look for a term for this activity, 'do it yourself' might seem an appropriate one. For the child itself gets up, balances, walks and falls – and neither mother nor father can do this for the child. Such 'do it yourself' activity plays a key role in more recent developmental theology, in which there are a variety of technical terms to describe it.[2]

Children at play are equally fascinating. When the Gulf War broke out in 1991 I watched a group of seven- and eight-year-old children piling up round blocks of wood into a tower. When it was finished, they knocked it down, producing a fearful noise. 'The bombs are falling, the bombs are falling,' they shouted, clearly infected by their parents' anxiety, and then began their symbolic game all over again. After a few more 'raids' they put the blocks of wood at the back of a shed, so that no one could drop any more bombs.

Apart from the cathartic effect – a diminution of anxiety – the following also took place in this game. The children developed new meanings *together* and gave these to the pieces of wood; for the children these *became* 'bombs'. The children developed new meaning, shared it, and in addition tacitly kept to rules: the tower could only be demolished when it was finished. All were agreed on that. Moreover one could even see the removal of the wood as a prophetic sign. According to this example, development takes place not only through the operations of the individual child but essentially in co-operation; as the psychologist J. Youniss put it, it is not just 'solitary' construction but shared 'co-construction'.[3] Here we have two key concepts of more recent developmental psychology: 'construction and co-construction'. Both concepts suggest seeing the child from the beginning as a subject; not just a monad and egocentric subject, but in principle a social subject.

But is it really appropriate to call the unweaned infant an 'active partner', to evaluate it as a 'social person'?[4] Doesn't everyday experience already teach us something else: the baby should be quiet, but it cries; it should drink, but its mouth will not grasp the nipple, and yet it begins to whimper and cry as soon as its mother puts it in the cot? Is that social? Isn't it rather selfishness, indeed wickedness, something which has still been attributed to the small child in this century, for example by Freud's pupil Glover, who regarded a 'normal small child' as 'thoroughly egocentric, greedy, dirty . . . and without any moral sensibility' and – as if that were not enough – branded it 'heedless, domineering and sadistic'?[5] Moreover, this pessimistic view of the child has prominent theological predecessors, especially Augustine, who wrote in his *Confessions*: 'No one is pure of sin before you, not even a small child who is no older than a day.'[6]

The same behaviour on the part of small children can lead to very different assessments by adults. These depend on what images or theories of the child are applied to it.[7] Certainly developmental psychology is based on anthropological presuppositions, which sometimes differ enormously and are subject to historical change; but it also has the task of making critical investigations and contributing empirical insights which at least bring us nearer to the real nature of the child. In this article I shall:
– contrast the view that children are primarily the products of upbringing and the environment with the view that they also form themselves;
– demonstrate that the wilfulness of the child which is so often contested in the history of upbringing can also be evaluated positively as the child having a mind of its own;
– challenge the image of the apparently irrational small child with results of research which justify the slogan 'the competent baby'.

Through all three areas runs the tension as to whether the child is seen as an object or a subject.

I Are children products of upbringing or do they form themselves?

If we are confronted with a person whose behaviour is striking, whether in person or through the media, we can hardly avoid the question 'How was he or she brought up?' This suggests that human beings – as Kant already claimed – are 'no more than education makes them',[8] and similarly that the child is a being which can be formed, an object like soft wax on which the environment in general and upbringing in particular stamps its seal. This view has a long tradition; it already occurs in the Middle Ages and antiquity, especially in Aristotle, but above all in Anglo-Saxon empiricism, which influenced developmental theology there and especially behaviourism. One of its most prominent representatives, John B. Watson, wrote: 'Give me a dozen healthy children and I guarantee that I can take one and make it a doctor, make another a lawyer, another an artist, another a merchant, another a beggar or a thief.'[9] Here the verb 'make' is revealing; applied to the child, it demotes it to an object which can be shaped at random. Behind this belief in the omnipotence of education lies the ideology of the possibility of unlimited planning and implementation which, following the Enlightenment and the technological revolution, did not stop short even at upbringing and the child.

But is the child more or less exclusively a product of upbringing? Church history in particular is rich in examples to the contrary. Giovanni Bernardone, whom his father, a rich cloth merchant, was accustomed to call 'Francesco', was born in Assisi in 1181. He was brought up to continue the family business and increase its wealth. But according to legend this child, brought up in such a way, threw the precious bolts of purple cloth out of the window and lived in poverty and for the poor. Even Rousseau, in his pedagogical classic *Emile*, thought the complete success of education impossible.[10]

The reason for this is that before educational measures take effect, they have to be perceived by the child. And the child does this in its own way. If a child is punished for disobedience, the punishment can lead it to see that it must be obedient. But another child who is punished for the same reason can feel confirmed in its assumption that its parents pay attention to it only when it goes against them – so it will go on doing so. In contrast to the assumptions of classic behaviourism, stimuli do not take place as such in the organism, but only when the organism accepts them, and moreover, only as the organism interprets them.[11] Perception and interpretation – usually called 'assimilation' in the cognitive psychology of development –

are always actions of the subject, and no one can take them away from the subject, not even the most benevolent education. So its limits are evident: 'There is no pedagogical system, however carefully devised, whose effects lead directly, i.e. solely, exclusively or predictably, to the results intended by pedagogy. In every case the autonomous self-authority in the child or young person stands in the middle.'[12]

Does that mean that upbringing should be abandoned completely, as some German and American educationalists are publicly advocating? Not at all! Upbringing works, perhaps not completely according to plan, but as far as the person being brought up accepts it. Often the child can only bow to the will of those who bring it up, especially when they behave autocratically and attach prime importance to breaking its stubbornness.

II From wilfulness to a mind of one's own

'Wilfulness' or its equivalents is one of the terms most used in the history of upbringing. For centuries the slogan was: 'The most important thing is for the natural will to be broken. This must be the main concern.' Thus August Hermann Francke at the beginning of the eighteenth century.[13] This wilfulness was thought already to show itself in the newborn child's cry of anger and was often explained as a direct manifestation of original sin. Countless stories of wilful children have been used for educational purposes, like the story of 'Ice Peter', told and illustrated by Wilhelm Busch. Peter wants to go ski-ing in the bitter cold despite his parents' warning. But he freezes on the lake, is found by his parents, and when taken into the warm inn melts down into slush.

But isn't the very word 'wilfulness' an indication that earlier generations, too, did not see the child just as a passive object? This question seems all the more important, since the thesis of Philippe Ariès that the distinctive nature of the child and childhood were largely unknown in the Middle Ages and discovered only at the beginning of modernity is still widespread – despite pertinent and convincing criticism.[14] Former generations, too, seem to have perceived that children are different: often stubborn, refractory, obstinate. The existence of a pedagogical slogan that the will must be broken if it will not bend presupposes a genuine will; the original subjectivity of the child, which, however, has been little empathized with, is to be domesticated so that it becomes an object.

It is to the credit of educational reform and developmental theology – which from the beginning have been closely allied – that they have seen the wilfulness of children in a positive light: as the child having a will of its own. It develops this will in interaction with the world in which it lives. To this degree the child is active and creative: in short, a subject. The vast amount of research into developmental psychology has convincingly shown that the child perceives things in its own way and reconstructs an independent view of the world. Piaget (1897–1981), who was probably the most significant developmental psychologist of the century, explicitly spoke of the 'construction of reality' by the child.[15] He described in minute detail how children build up cognitive structures by their action, how they develop the concepts of number and space, or how they construct their concept of time. Initially time is in no way an abstract series of intervals but identical with concrete events, so that younger children can only ask, 'How many times do I have to go to sleep before my birthday?' In the meantime moral development has also been seen in essentially a more differentiated way than in the traditional view, according to which a distinction between good and evil could be made from the age of seven onwards; children clearly develop this capacity earlier and it leads to the 'moral universe' characteristic of them in which the 'goodies' and the 'baddies' are fixed precisely – as in fairy stories or films like Batman.

The veils which lay over the religious conceptions of children have also been removed, at least in part. In his theory of the development of religious judgment, Fritz Oser has shown how children structure their relationship with God when they have to cope with contingent events in life. To begin with they think that it is almost impossible to influence God; then they assume that God's attitude depends on what human beings do.[16] It has repeatedly been demonstrated that younger children tend towards anthropomorphic images of God, that most of them locate 'God' up in heaven; he has to be able to look down on them.[17]

Equally well known are their artificial models of interpretation according to which even natural things like mountains have been 'made', and trees for human beings 'so that they have something to eat'. Younger children also still find it difficult to see through the symbolic or metaphorical structure of religious language: they understand it literally and in a concrete way, and this often leads to confusions, like: 'God has lived with us!' 'That's not true – it was the Smiths!' Sometimes they arrive at particularly original interpretations of parables like the parable of the lost sheep in Luke 15.3–7. In a primary class the teacher explained that it was a picture of how Jesus cares for each of us equally. But when a pupil was asked about it later, she saw it like this: 'Once Jesus looked after 100 sheep; one ran away and he went after it and found it and was glad.' However, this incompletely developed understanding of metaphorical language is as it were compensated for by a less problematical access to the world of fantasy and symbol, which can perform important hygienic functions for psychology.[18]

There is an obvious objection: children merely reflect 'theological ideas' and reproduce what they have heard from their parents or elsewhere. This objection is often made and betrays an image of the child to match: passive, influenced and in no way having its own independent theological competence. The fact that childish notions, for example those of a five-year-old, are simply too original for this explanation, tells against this. 'God must have made the world in a day; in the evening he wouldn't have been able to see clearly enough.' Or who would have taught children to say that God made the first cars and clocks 'for people to see how things were going'?

Small children also already articulate their own views in their questions: 'Why don't we see two things with two eyes?'[19] '"Is God a boy or a girl?", "No", "Then something in between?"'[20] Karl Jaspers reckoned that children's questions were 'a marvellous sign that human beings as such originally philosophize . . . Quite often one hears from the lips of children things which go to the depths of philosophy.'[21] 'Children's philosophy' has now found a following.[22] It would not have been possible without the removal of the negative picture of the child according to which the child is irrational, foolish and given over to its passions – thus no less a figure than Aristotle, who mentioned 'small children' and 'wild animals' in the same breath.

It is time for theology to follow philosophy here and equally allow a theology *of* children, not a theology *about* children, which often betrays more the romantic projections and wishes of grown-ups. It needs to be a theology which frankly and freely comes from the lips of children. In an essay on 'What would you ask the Pope?', a ten-year-old boy from Naples wrote: 'Whether he was a fan of Italy or Poland. And I would also like to know who hears his confession.'[23] What grown-up talks like this – as disarmingly as the child in 'The Emperor's New Clothes'?

III 'Unconscious organisms' or 'competent babies'?

Probably the most convincing evidence that children are subjects has been produced by more recent research into small children. William James, one of the founding fathers of American psychology, still regarded small children as 'unconscious organisms, largely without feeling, unreceptive and incapable of learning'.[24] Classical psychoanalysis passed a similarly pessimistic judgment on the child: according to Freud it is 'amoral, it has no inner inhibitions about its impulses which strive for pleasure';[25] in the oral and anal phases it is at the mercy of the id, because the ego is still very weak. Granted, later psychoanalysis toned down this conflictual view of the child's experience, but the deficiency remained: according to Margreth Mahler the baby in the first weeks of life is 'in a state of hallucinatory disorientation' and then – around six to seven months – enters the normal symbiotic phase, though it still has 'no concept, no scheme of itself and others' and thus no subjectivity.[26]

Newer methods of obtaining data – especially with video recordings – have revolutionized the picture of the small child. Daniel Stern was a pioneer: on the basis of intensive and precise observations, along with his great gift for empathy, he described four stages of sense of self in the very first year of life.[27]

In the first weeks of life, the baby actively develops a sense of its emerging self. It already tends to make relationships between different events with the help of innate capacities. Its capacities for sensual perception have also been underestimated: children three weeks old who sucked a burled dummy with a blindfold looked more intensely at this when the blindfold was taken off than at a dummy with a smooth surface. Evidently they are capable of sensory co-ordinations, i.e. they can relate different modes of sensing (seeing, touching) to a single object: this already makes possible a coherent perception of the world at an age at which, according to earlier views, sense impressions would throng in on them in a confused and chaotic way.

Between the third and eighth months of life the small child develops the 'core self'. It is already aware that it and the person to whom it relates are physically separate entities. Thus the concept of a symbiosis in which there is no 'I' proves questionable. Stern also attests in babies origination, i.e. the sense of originating their own actions and not originating the actions of others: possessing wills, being able to control actions which they initiate themselves. If they are disturbed in their activities (for example, touched), they react in an annoyed way and try to complete the activity successfully. To experience oneself as author of one's own actions is a characteristic of subjectivity.

The description of phase three, which begins in the eighth month of life and lasts up to the age of fifteen to eighteen months, speaks explicitly of a 'subjective sense of self'. The small child becomes aware that the inward subjective experiences, the content of its feelings and thoughts can in some circumstances be shared by others. It is precisely in this that inter-subjectivity consists; and it first becomes possible when a subject is both aware of itself and can perceive the subjectivity of the other. This is not possible without a minimum number of shared symbols like gestures or sounds, which make possible the 'intentional communality' which forms the basis of learning to talk. Moments in which the attention of mother/ father and child are directed to the same object and this is named are decisive.

The fourth phase is a verbal sense of self which in principle remains incomplete. Now the child can begin to construct the narrative of its own life. Inter-subjectivity is facilitated and at the same time extended on the basis of language – which is shared meaning *par excellence*. At the same time the child forms the capacity to 'objectivize' itself, for example in symbolic play, in which even two-year-olds can depict in scenes their own anxieties and wishes. For the first time the child is in a position to oppose a clearly outlined wish to reality as it actually presents itself. That, too, is subjectivity.

The Romans called children up to the age of around seven *infantes*, i.e. beings which do not speak. More recent research into children has shown just how untenable this view is. Traditional developmental psychology has also evidently had a tendency to underestimate children, and has often regarded them from the perspective of what they are not yet able to do. Quite a different picture emerges if what they can already do in the very first months of life is evaluated: a tremendous amount! And this becomes completely mysterious in the positive sense when one reflects what rapid progress they make in only a short time in the spheres of mobility, cognition and communication.

There is one thing that we can say with full justification: those who see children primarily as objects or empty vessels which can only be filled by adults, or think that they merely have to be brought up, have the whole of more recent child research against them. 'Babies are wiser.'[28] Moreover, small children in particular influence the behaviour of adults, especially parents, to a much greater degree than these are usually conscious of. A small child laughs at an adult and the corners of the adult's mouth turn up in pleasure. A one-year-old sits opposite its mother and waves its rattle vigorously up and down: the mother involuntarily nods her head in time. Stern speaks of tuning the emotions, in a way which happens as it were pre-consciously and guarantees a deep inter-subjectivity that precedes language and can hardly be put into words.

If babies are evidently active subjects, then so too are pre-school and school children who come into contact with religious education and the church. But often these are seen as religious 'clean sheets', the offshoots of secular families including the religiously illiterate to whom the elements of the faith must be communicated – in the first instance 'systematically' and 'completely'. The thesis formulated by the Fulda Bishops' Conference in 1924 arguing against the idea of 'heuristic schools' is typical of this view of religious education: it is 'the task of catechists as messengers of God to bring children to the substance of faith, not the task of children to work it out'.[29] Anyone who approaches children with this attitude – which is again gaining approval in conservative church circles – is by-passing the children and missing something very important and indeed rejuvenating: learning from children!

Translated by John Bowden

Notes

1. A key book in my studies was N. Mette, *Voraussetzungen christlicher Elementarerziehung. Vorbereitende Studien zu einer Religionspädagogik des Kleinkindalters*, Düsseldorf 1984.
2. Already A. Petzelt, *Kindheit – Jugend – Reifezeit. Grundriss der Phasen psychischer Entwicklung*, Freiburg im Breisgau 1961, esp. 20f. Some introductions to recent psychology of development are: R. Oerter and L. Montada, *Entwicklungspsychologie. Ein Lehrbuch*, Munich [3]1995; H. M. Trautner, *Lehrbuch der Entwicklungspsychologie* (2 vols.), Göttingen 1991/92; A. Flammer, *Entwicklungstheorien. Psychologische Theorien der menschlichen Entwicklung*, Bern, etc. 1988.
3. J. Youniss, *Soziale Konstruktion und psychische Entwicklung*, Frankfurt am Main 1994.
4. Thus W. Damon, *Die Soziale Entwicklung des Kindes. Ein entwicklungspsychologisches Lehrbuch*, Stuttgart 1989, 40f.
5. Quoted from A. Montagu, *Zum Kind reifen*, Stuttgart 1984, 164.
6. Augustine, *Confessions*, 38.
7. H. Scholz, *Die Konstruktion des Kindes. Über Kinder und Kindheit*, Opladen 1994.
8. I. Kant, *Über Pädagogik*, A 7.
9. From D. Elkind, *Das gehetzte Kind*, Hamburg 1991, 40.
10. J. J. Rousseau, *Émile*, Harmondsworth 1991.
11. This is a basic assumption of psychology after its 'cognitive shift'; H. Gardner, *Dem Denken auf der Spur, Der Weg der Kognitionswissenschaft*, Stuttgart 1992.
12. O. Speck, *Chaos und Autonomie in der Erziehung*, Munich and Basel 1991, 130.
13. A. H. Francke, *Werke in Auswahl*, ed. E. Peschke, Berlin 1969, 126; there are further documents in K. Rutschky, *Schwarze Pädagogik. Quellen zur Naturgeschichte bürgerlicher Erziehung*, Frankfurt am Main etc. 1977.
14. P. Ariès, *Centuries of Childhood*, London 1962; S. Shahar, *Kindheit im Mittelalter*, Munich and Zurich 1991, is critical.

15. J. Piaget, *The Language and Thought of the Child*, London ³1989; id., *The Child's Conception of the World*, New York 1983.

16. F. Oser and P. Gmünder, *Der Mensch – Stufen seiner religiösen Entwicklung*, Gütersloh ³1992.

17. A. Bucher, 'Alter Gott zu neuen Kindern? Neue Gott von alten Kindern? Was sind 343 Kinder unter Gott vorstellen?', in V. Merz (ed.), *Alter Gott für neue Kinder?*, Fribourg 1994, 79–100.

18. See B. Bettelheim, *Ein Leben für Kinder*, Munich 1990, 388–423.

19. From M. Doehlemann, *Die Phantasie der Kinder und was Erwachsene daraus lernen können*, Frankfurt am Main 1985, 54.

20. From J. Klink, *Your Child and Religion*, London 1972, 88.

21. K. Jaspers, *Was ist Philosophie? Ein Lesebuch*, Munich 1975, 34.

22. H. L. Freese, *Kinder sind Philosophen*, Weinheim 1989.

23. From M. D'Orte (ed.), *Gott hat uns alle gratis erschaffen. Schulaufsätze neapolitanischer Kinder*, Zurich 1993, 193.

24. From H. Trotter, 'Babies sind klüger', in Psychologie heute (ed.), *Klein sein, gross werden*, Weinheim 1989, 7–20: 8.

25. S. Freud, *Introductory Lectures on Psychoanalysis*, Harmondsworth 1991, 500.

26. M. Mahler et al., *Die psychische Geburt des Menschen*, Frankfurt am Main 1980, 60, 68.

27. For what follows, see D. Stern, *The Interpersonal World of the Infant*, New York 1985; cf. also M. Dornes, *Der kompetente Säugling. Die präverbale Entwicklung des Menschen*, Frankfurt am Main 1993.

28. Cf. n. 24.

29. From H. Fox, *Kompendium Didaktik: Katholische Religion*, Munich 1986, 149.

Children in Matthew: A Semantic Study

Wim Weren

I Introduction

In the Gospels, all kinds of figures appear who are like people in our world. So it is not surprising that these books often speak of children. The best known story is the one in which Jesus, despite criticism from his disciples, emerges as a friend of children (Matt. 19. 13–15; Mark 10. 13–16; Luke 18. 15–17). This story is very like another story in which Jesus uses a child as a model for his disciples when they are quarrelling over the question which of them is the most important (Matt. 18 1–5; Mark 9. 33–37; Luke 9. 46–48). However, this is far from being a complete list. The Gospels contain a number of other texts on children.

How do these texts function in exegesis? They have often been investigated by means of diachronic (= 'through time') methods.[1] Diachronic exegesis of texts primarily investigates the stages of development which a text has gone through before taking its final form.[2]

Other exegetes prefer to examine texts in their final form. They increasingly make use of synchronic (= contemporaneous) methods. These are not very interested in the development which the text has undergone but rather with the structures and lines of meaning which can be perceived within a particular text.

In this article I have opted for the second approach. I shall apply it to texts from Matthew. His book is full of stories and texts about children. I shall develop some of them in a semantic analysis. Not all these texts have a parallel in Mark or Luke. But even texts which Matthew has in common with Mark or Luke must primarily be read within their own literary context.

II Children in Matthew 2

The first child encountered by the reader of Matthew is Jesus himself. In 2.1 he is called by the name which Joseph has given him on the instructions of an angel (1.21, 25), and which in brief describes his life's work: he is to save his people from their sins. In the rest of Matt. 2, Jesus is constantly referred to as 'the child': nine times in all (2.8, 9, 11, 13, 14, 20, 21). It is striking that this child is exclusively associated with his mother. Although Joseph immediately recognizes the child as his own, we constantly find the phrase 'the child and his mother' (2.11, 13, 14, 20, 21). In this way the reader is reminded of the special origin of Jesus, which is described at length in Matt. 1. He is born of Mary, but her husband is not the physical father of Jesus. The obvious thought that in that case he must have been born as a result of an affair between Mary and another man is vigorously rejected in 1.18–25. What is special about Jesus is that he is born of Mary 'and of the Holy Spirit'. He is not a child like other children. This is further underlined by the quotation from Hos. 11.1 which the narrator in 2.15 inserts into his own story and which is presented as a saying of God himself: 'Out of Egypt I have called my son' (cf. 3.17; 12.18; 17.5).

The child himself plays a passive role. This accords with his age; he has only just been born and in any case is not yet two years old. Moreover the course of the action is completely dominated by other figures: by the magi, by Herod and Joseph, and above all by God, who is the real power behind the story related here, even if he does not appear directly on stage. God makes use of angels to influence the course of things: Joseph's dreams and the star which guides the magi cannot be detached from God's sphere of influence. The story which is told follows a particular scenario which is prefigured in scripture. The quotations relating to the fulfilment of prophecies emphasize that the story of Jesus is a recapitulation of what happened to Israel.

It is evident from the scripture that the child is the leader who comes from Bethlehem, the shepherd of Israel, modelled on David. Later in Matthew it will become clear that leaders of the community must model themselves on children: here someone who is still a child is depicted as a leader. The magi call him 'the king of the Jews' (v. 2), a term which a few verses later Herod turns into 'the messiah' (v. 4). Before Jesus himself is in action or has even spoken a word, his life is threatened: King Herod seeks to kill the child. The story about his earliest youth is already a passion narrative in a nutshell. But here, too, it has also already become clear that Jesus enjoys God's protection and that he will emerge victorious from the dispute.

Jesus is not the only child in Matt. 2. The story also speaks of other children, contemporaries of Jesus. Herod has them killed in cold blood in an action which is really directed against his messianic rival. The narrator connects the massacre in Bethlehem with the sorry fate of Rachel's children, who are deported to Babylon (Jer. 31.15). Here too history repeats itself, but now in all its cruelty: children lose their lives in an orgy of violence. The quotation about the fulfilment of prophecy is not introduced here with a final clause ('that it might be fulfilled'), but with a chronological note ('then it was fulfilled'). The event described is certainly in accord with scripture, but it is so terrible that the narrator does not formulate the connection with scripture as he does elsewhere in his book (cf. also 27.9f.). Evidently he wants to indicate in this way that the violence of which the children of Bethlehem have become the victims is not the work of God but finds its origin in human actions.

III Children as recipients of revelation

In Matt. 11 Jesus twice compares his hearers with children, in 11.16f. and 11.25. In 11.16 he has negative characteristics of children in view: they quarrel with one another while playing in the market place. In 11.25 he speaks in positive terms of the smallest children: 'I thank you, Father, Lord of heaven and earth, because you have hidden these things from the wise and understanding and revealed them to babes.' The Greek here is *nepioi*. Starting from the fact that small children still live on their mothers' milk (Heb. 5.13), that they are far from being grown up (I Cor. 13.11), and that they have the same lowly position as slaves within the household (Gal. 4.1), *nepioi* is used to denote adults who are just converted. *Nepioi* also has a figurative sense in Matt. 11.25. Children there are recipients of God's revelation. Jesus is referring to his disciples and contrasting them with the wise and understanding. In doing so he picks up a characteristic of children which often emerges in texts from the ancient world:[4] children have not yet received any schooling; they still have to be initiated into the world of adults. The smallest of them are called by Jesus, who is Wisdom in his own person, to come to him (cf. 19.14, 'let the children come to me', see also Sir. 29.19f.) and learn from him. They are particularly good at learning the Torah from him, while the wise and understanding are hampered by the knowledge that they already have. Under the surface we can detect here criticism of apocalyptic seers who claim to have secret revelations of which the great mass of people knows nothing. However, it is precisely this last group which has been mobilized by Jesus. He promises them that they will find rest with him. This term, too, has apocalyptic colouring: eschatological salvation is often described as 'rest' (cf. Heb. 3.7–4.11).

Later in Matthew we find two texts which develop 11.25. The first is 16.17. There Jesus says that Peter does not have himself to thank for his insight that Jesus is the Messiah, the Son of God, but that God has revealed this to him. By this characterization, Peter, an adult, is given a place among the 'babes' in 11.25. It is interesting that the knowledge which people receive from God can again be eclipsed by their own notions. Immediately after his confession Peter shows himself to be a declared opponent of the idea that Jesus will have to suffer and die. In so doing he reveals himself as the Satan who seeks to deter Jesus from his God-given task.

Matthew 21.14–17 is the second text which develops 11.25. Immediately after his entry into Jerusalem, Jesus goes to the temple, where he attacks the commercial activities around the sacrificial cult and heals the blind and the cripples. While he does this, small children are standing in the temple courts shouting 'Hosanna to the Son of David' (cf. 21.9). The high priests and scribes get worked up about this and speak to Jesus about the uproar which he has caused. Not without sarcasm he asks his opponents whether they have ever read scripture (cf. 12.3, 5; 19.4). He refers them to Ps. 8.3: 'Out of the mouths of babes and sucklings you have ordained praise.' The quotation is taken from the Septuagint version. The psalm begins and ends with the same sentence: 'O, Lord, how marvellous (*thaumaston*) is your name over all the earth' (vv. 2.8). This sentence is echoed in Matt. 21.14, which speaks of the marvellous things (*thaumasia*) that Jesus did. Later the psalm claims that God has put praise in the mouths of children to put his enemies to shame. This story of Matthew's reflects the attitudes in the psalm very precisely: small children adore Jesus through God's doing, while the temple aristocracy are hostile to him.

IV Children in Matthew 18

Matthew 18 contains words of Jesus which are addressed to the disciples and are provoked by their question about who is the greatest in the kingdom of heaven. What Jesus says to them is divided into two parts, 18.1–20 and 18.21–35. Between v. 20 and v. 21 there is a break, because the speaker is interrupted at this point by Peter, who puts a question to him. The first part of what Jesus says is particularly interesting in connection with my theme. The structure of this part is as follows:[5]

A	18.1–4	Question of the disciples: 'Who is the greatest in the kingdom of heaven?'
B	18.5–20	Tensions in the community
X		18.5–9 Giving offence (negative)
Y		18.10–14 Parable of the stray sheep
X'		18.15–20 Reconciliation (positive).

Sub-section A is framed by the question of the disciples (v. 1) and Jesus' answer to it (v. 4). The question and the answer are carefully balanced (v. 1: 'Who is the greatest in the kingdom of heaven?'; v. 4: 'He is the greatest in the kingdom of heaven'). The unity of vv. 1–4 further emerges from the word 'child' or 'children' (vv. 2, 3, 4). As a preparation to his answer to the disciples Jesus puts a child in their midst (v. 2). He follows up this action with two sayings, the first of which is put in negative terms (v. 3) and the second positively (v. 4).

In favour of separating off sub-section B (vv. 5–20) is the fact that the name of Jesus is mentioned at the beginning and the end (vv. 5, 20, 'in my name'). These verses are also connected by Jesus' identification of himself in v. 5 with 'one such child' and his assurance in v. 20 that he is present where two or three are gathered in his name. Two expressions, each of which occurs three times, function as key words in sub-section B: 'one of these little ones' (vv. 6, 10, 14) and 'my (or your) Father in heaven' (vv. 10, 14, 19).

Sub-section B consists of three sub-units. Verses 5–9 are made into a tight unit by the key word 'cause to sin' and the agreement between 'one such child' (v. 5) and 'one of these little ones' (v. 6). The second sub-unit (vv. 10–14) consists of the parable of the stray sheep (vv. 12–13) surrounded by two sentences which are arranged in a chiastic order:

| v. 10 | A | one of these little ones | B my Father in heaven |
| v. 14 | B' | your Father in heaven | A' one of these little ones. |

The third sub-unit (vv. 15–20) mentions an interaction between two or three community members (v. 15, 'between you and him alone'; v. 16, 'take one or two others along . . . two or three witnesses'; v. 19, 'two of you'; 'two or three').

We now turn to the lines of meaning in 18.1–20. One of the threads which runs through the text can be shown as follows:

child (vv. 2, 3, 4) → such a child (v. 5) → one of these little ones (vv. 6, 10, 14).

The elements in this series are interconnected but are not synonyms. I shall examine them one by one.

In v. 2 Jesus performs a symbolic action: in order to make it clear what attitude he expects from his disciples, he puts a child in their midst. According to Jesus, that child is a living illustration of the ethical standards by which the disciples must act. Unless they become like children, they will not enter the kingdom of God; and the one who humbles himself (*tapeinosei heauton*) will be the greatest in the kingdom of heaven (cf. 23.12). What is expected of the disciples is not shown only by the child that Jesus put in their midst. According to 11.29, Jesus himself also functions as an ethical paradigm: he is lowly of heart (*tapeinos tē kardiā*). The disciples are to be seen to be like Jesus. Thus Jesus and the child both serve as living illustrations of the way the disciple must take. They must break with prevailing patterns of behaviour and voluntarily take the lowest place in the community.

The question now is how v. 5, in which the word 'child' appears again, follows on from vv. 1–4. This verse can be interpreted in two ways. It is arguable that the word 'child' still has a literal meaning even in v. 5, and refers back to the child in v. 2 who is presented as a model for the disciples. In that case v. 5 speaks of children who depend on the help of others; the disciples must follow them in this. Here we are to think above all of orphans. The care of this group is always a high priority in scripture (cf. Exod. 22. 22–24; Deut. 24. 19–21; Isa. 1.17; Ezek.22.7; Ps. 68.6) and is thought so important by Jesus that he identifies completely with it (those who accept such a child into his home accept Jesus).

A second interpretation is possible, and this can be indicated as follows. In v. 5 there is a subtle shift with important consequences for meaning. After v. 4 ('this child'), v. 5 speaks of 'one such child', a phrase which need not necessarily be taken literally but can also be understood figuratively. In this case the syntagma relates to followers of Jesus who put the word of vv. 3–4 into practice. These are disciples who have become 'as children' for the sake of the kingdom, in other words, who have opted for a vulnerable and marginal position in society. According to v. 5 they have to be supported by those around them. Their option is so valued by Jesus that he gathers them as a following and regards good deeds done for this group as being connected with himself.

I prefer this second interpretation. 'One such child' is another link in the chain; this expression makes a bridge between 'child' in vv. 2–4 and 'one of these little ones' in vv. 6, 10, 14. This idea of the place and function of v. 5 is confirmed by the contrasts between this verse and the next verse:

v. 5 Whoever receives one such child in my name → positive sanction;
v. 6 But whoever causes one of these little ones to sin → negative sanction.

Both these verses speak of a special group in the community and they fix attention on the way in which this group is treated by other members of the community; whereas v. 5 speaks of positive reactions of people round about them, v. 6 is about negative actions of which they are the target.

The next problem is the precise meaning of 'one of these little ones'. This combination of words occurs in 10.42 as well as in 18.6, 10, 13; we also find a superlative ('the least of these') in 25.40, 45. This combination of words does not have the same meaning everywhere. The meaning is sometimes dependent on the context. In 10.42 'the little ones' serves as a description of the twelve disciples who have been sent out by Jesus: they are dependent on the hospitality of others, since they may not make any material provision for their travels. In 25.40, 45 'the least of these' refers to someone who – for whatever reason – is hungry and thirsty, has no clothes, is a stranger, sick or in prison. The idea that the little ones do not have the material means necessary to keep them alive is not completely absent from 18.5–14 either (cf. v. 5), but this text provides a number of other elements for determining their identity.

To begin with, it is quite clear that the passage is about disciples of Jesus. This can be inferred from the periphrasis in v. 6, 'one of these little ones who believe in me'. But there is no reason here to think only of the twelve apostles (as in 10.42) or to regard the 'little ones' as a designation of all disciples. Of course all disciples are called on to put into practice the ideal formulated in vv. 2–4, but vv. 5–13 show that only a limited group actually follows the ideal and that these people are being prevented by people from their circle who do not make the same choice. I think that I can substantiate this view from the negative activities which are mentioned in the text. The little ones encounter a good deal of enmity: people try to cause them to sin and look down on them in a condescending way. The effect of this is that they begin to distance themselves from the community and risk being eliminated. The threats against them partly come from their fellow-believers and are in sharp contrast to the respect that God has for them. At whatever cost, the Father in heaven will not let them be lost. His special care for the little ones must be a stimulus to the community to give a proper place to their itinerant life.

This description of the little ones is based on the following observations. The group is discussed not only in v. 6 but also in vv. 10–14. The parable of the stray sheep (vv. 12–13) specifically refers to their situation. This emerges both from the sentences with which it is framed (vv. 10, 14) and also from the emphasis that the parable itself puts on the fate of one stray sheep from a large flock (v. 12: 'one of them' – it is no coincidence that the number comes first!). This one sheep is not lost (as it is in Luke 15.3–7) but it has strayed. The term 'stray' is preferred here three times, and also occurs (though in the active, 'lead astray') in the description of the appearance of false prophets and false messiahs in 24.4f., 11,24. There is a second connection with eschatological discourse, namely the phrase 'cause to sin' (18.6–9) or 'fall away' (24.10). Both passages speak about division in the community. The malaise is caused by members in positions of leadership. By being too concerned with their own position in exercising this function and not realizing that leadership implies service, they make victims in their own circle. In eschatological discourse it is those faithful to the law (24.12) and even the elect (24.24) who risk becoming the victims of internal tensions. In 18.5–14 it is precisely the members of the community who have attached great importance to Jesus' ideal who have got into trouble.

V Children in Matthew 19.13–15

This well-known passage describes how children are brought to Jesus for him to lay hands on them. In the end he does precisely what is expected of him, and indeed lays hands on the children. We are not told who bring the children to Jesus. Moreover, the disciples are scandalized by the children themselves and not with the adults who bring them into contact with Jesus. Thus the number of those involved is limited to three: Jesus, the disciples and the children. The disciples are told that they must stop their opposition. This call is explained in the closing words of v. 14: 'for of such children is the kingdom of heaven'. In this context the word 'children' has a figurative meaning. The phrase is 'such children' (or 'such people') and not 'these children'.

Matthew 19.13–15 must be read against the background of Gen. 48, where Jacob on his deathbed pronounces his blessing over Ephraim and Manasseh, the two sons of Joseph.[6] The two texts have various elements in common: (a) the children are brought to Joseph (Gen. 48.10,13) or

Jesus (Matt. 19.13); (b) there is mention of the laying on of hands (Gen. 48.10; Matt. 19.13,15); (c) this gesture is coupled with a prayer (Gen. 48.15–16; Matt. 19,15). In Genesis the natural hierarchy plays a major role. Joseph respects this hierarchy by putting Manasseh, the oldest, on the right hand of his father and Ephraim on his left. But Jacob blesses the pair with arms crossed, so that the youngest really receives the blessing that was intended for the firstborn. This reversal of existing conditions is also echoed in Matt. 19.13–15, in two respects: (a) Jesus' solidarity with children (vv. 14a, 15) is in tension with the view of his time that young children occupy the lowest place on the social ladder; (b) by his metaphorical use of the term 'children' (v. 14b), Jesus indicates that for the sake of the kingdom his disciples must break with the conventional hierarchy of values in their environment and must opt for a life which is characterized by vulnerability.

VI Conclusion

So what is the significance of the term 'child' in Matthew? This word is rendered by different terms in the Greek text (*paidion, pais, teknon, nepios*). In a number of texts it denotes real children. They form a vulnerable group, which is dependent on the care of parents (7.11); the dark side of this that they are involved in the miserable circumstances of their parents (18.25) or become the victims of negative options on the part of adults (2.16–18; 27.24). They are exposed to sickness (8.5–13; 9.2, 18–19, 23–26; 15.21–28; 17.14–18) and suffer hunger (14.21; 15.38). Matthew also has an eye for the negative characteristics of children: they are fickle (11.16) and oppose their parents (10.21). Children can count on Jesus' sympathy (19.13–15) and he even urges his followers to take great care of them (18.5). Half of the texts in which the term 'child' (*paidion*) occurs relate to Jesus himself. He is a special child who is born 'of the Holy Spirit' and is protected by God from those who lie in wait for him. From the beginning, the narrative in Matt. 2 gives the word 'child' a definite semantic colouring. Some aspects of this recur when 'child' is used in a metaphorical sense and applied to (certain) followers of Jesus. They are the ones who receive God's blessing and are initiated into the Torah by Jesus (11.25–30). Emphasis is put on the fact that God shows a special concern for vulnerable members of the community of faith, for the 'little ones'. In 10.42 this term relates to the Twelve in their missionary role, in 18.6–14 to believers who are treated with contempt by other members of the community – above all by its leaders – and therefore risk being alienated from the community. The presupposition of the saying that followers of Jesus must become children is not that children by definition have positive qualities (like innocence, receptiveness), though it cannot be denied that the positive statement in 18.4 (whoever becomes like this child does this) supports such interpretations. However, this verse has primarily another significance. It indicates that children occupy the lowest position in society and that it is evident that this position must also be characteristic of those who see the kingdom of heaven as the supreme value.

Translated by John Bowden

Notes

1. E.g. S. Légasse, *Jésus et l'enfant. 'Enfants', 'petits' et 'simple' dans la tradition synoptique*, Études bibliques, Paris 1969; G. Krause (ed.), *Die Kinder im Evangelium*, Stuttgart and Göttingen 1973.

2. In the case of Mark 10.13–16 this approach leads to the following results. Following Bultmann (*The History of the Synoptic Tradition*, Oxford 1963, 32), it is generally assumed that v. 15 is secondary. At any rate this logion is in tension with the saying in v. 14. The rest of the passage (vv. 13, 16) has the form of a biographical apophthegm which has been formed by the community, perhaps on the basis of recollections of a striking event from Jesus' life or on the basis of an authentic saying of Jesus about the special relationship between children and the kingdom of God. That the tradition preserved here is a 'community construction' is evident from the fact that participation in the kingdom of God is put in the perspective of entering into a relationship with Jesus, and this points to a christology which presumably developed only within the community. It is also important that the text speaks of a conflict between Jesus and his disciples. That conflict reflects a discussion in the community which could be resolved only with an appeal to Jesus. What specific question this discussion was about is not easy to determine, because the word 'children' can be understood both literally and figuratively. If the discussion was about real children, one could assume that questions had arisen in the community at an early stage about whether young children could be admitted to baptism or the catechumenate (e.g. A. Lindemann, 'Die Kinder und die Gottesherrschaft. Markus 10.13–16 und die Stellung der Kinder in der späthellenistischer Gesellschaft und im Urchristentum', in H. P. Stähli [ed.], *Wort und Dienst. Jahrbuch der Kirchlichen Hochschule Bethel*, Neue Folge 17, Bielefeld 1983, 77–104). The question is given a positive answer in our text with a reference to Jesus. If one opts for a figurative meaning of 'the children' and relates the term to certain (adult) members of the community of faith, then one could think of itinerant prophets (see G. Ringshausen, 'Die Kinder der Weisheit. Zur Auslegung von Mk 10, 13–16 par.', *Zeitschrift für die neutestamentliche Wissenschaft* 77, 1986, 34–63). The text would then be a criticism of the inhospitable and intolerant attitude of certain local communities towards this group.

3. P. Müller, *In der Mitte der Gemeinde. Kinder im Neuen Testament*, Neukirchen-Vluyn 1992, applies both diachronic and synchronic methods; he also combines his exegesis with practical theology.

4. See Lindemann, 'Die Kinder' (n. 2), 81–88; Müller, *In der Mitte* (n. 3), 81–164, 'Kinder in der Umwelt des Neuen Testaments'.

5. W. G. Thompson, *Matthew's Advice to a Divided Community. Mt 17,22–18, 35*, Analecta Biblica 44, Rome 1970.

6. See J. Duncan M. Derrett, 'Why Jesus Blessed the Children (Mark 10.13–16 par.)', *Novum Testamentum* 25, 1983, 1–18.

Fides Infantium – A Conversion

Dieter Seiler

Introduction

For me, the content of this article represents a turning point in my own theoretical and practical work: encounter with the small child and its faith. This encounter has been extensive, varied and yet limited: in practice as a father with children of my own, as a pastor and teacher in the local community, and as a therapist in reconstructing childhood in psychoanalysis and in the form of recollections of my own childhood. In the theoretical sphere, there are Sigmund Freud and more recent authors on psychoanalysis, and the whole science of human ethology with the observation of babies which has now opened up. As a further source, I am thinking of some great theologians who have recalled their childhood and made it the foundation of their theological thought, of Augustine and Martin Luther with his independent idea of *fides infantium*, which has not really been taken in even today. I am keeping to this Latin term because it bears no similarity to what today is called 'the child's faith'.

We live today with an oppressive contradiction: we idealize children and childhood and at the same time let millions of children go to waste, physically, spiritually and intellectually. We start something here and become its helpless victims. The idealizing is only one particular way of exploiting children for the feelings of adults. Habit is just the other side of a tendency to neglect. Our relationship with the child is deeply disturbed, and as a result so is our relationship to other men and women and to ourselves. Our relationship to the child is disturbed because even in the churches – indeed particularly in the churches – we regard the child as the object of upbringing and teaching and not as the subject of its own experiences which are not directly accessible to us. We teach and expect 'faith'. Implicitly or explicitly, the churches have the view that they are in possession of the substance of faith, which they hand down in teaching so that faith arises.

The English psychoanalyst Donald W. Winnicott dedicates his last work to the children 'from whom I have learned'. This is to be understood not just as a sentimental gesture but as a principle of research. In their therapeutic practice, Winnicott and others have shared through small children in insights which are related to the basic elements of human spiritual life. Winnicott feels that he is not primarily a helper and a doctor but a researcher, who is trying to understand something which concerns him most deeply. I would not hesitate to put this attitude in parallel with Jesus' attitude to the children in the Gospel. And I only hope that the practice and theory of the church and theology adopts a similar attitude to faith: discovering elements of faith in the perception of small children.

Developmental psychology: what are we talking about when we say 'faith'?

Many of us pastoral psychologists began to form such an insight through the work of Erik Erikson. Taking up Freud's discovery of the drives, he outlined a scheme of human psycho-social development in eight steps, which begins with the primal situation, the scene depicted so often in our tradition: the mother and the small child. We learned from Erikson that this primal situation provides decisive foundations for the further formation of the inner human world. Erikson speaks of primal trust which is taken up by, for example, religious institutions.

In the 1980s, two works appeared in professional psychoanalytical literature in which the author Michael Eigen concerned himself with 'faith' in relation to small children. They caused a stir, since hitherto psychoanalysis in the tradition of Sigmund Freud had been strongly critical of religion. Religion appeared as a collective neurosis with a compulsive character. Only a few theologians like the Swiss Reformed pastor Oscar Pfister had been able to build a bridge between the two disciplines. But from the beginning psychoanalysis was concerned with investigating childhood through the reconstruction of children's experiences and through direct observation.

Most recently, psychoanalytic concepts relating to the small chlid have been investigated by human ethology. Babies have been observed in very sophisticated experiments, and it has proved that they are very purposive beings who have basic impulses which are also fundamental in adult life. I see them as being basic elements of what is meant by faith, *fides*.

Fides infantium – just a reminiscence, or a discovery?

It was Martin Luther who first attributed *fides*, faith, to small children, primarily in connection with the doctrine of baptism. Since Augustine it had been held that the faith of the recipient was a necessary part of the valid reception of the sacrament. This can be shown in all sacraments, but not in infant baptism: should small children themselves already believe? How can one imagine that? Traditional church doctrine saw the faith of parents and above all of the church as a substitute for the lack of faith in the child, so in this view church and parents functioned vicariously for the child with their adult faith, and through education and doctrine led it to believe. Luther, for whom *fides* represented a central personal orientation, had to oppose this. He found himself fighting on two fronts: over against tradition he called for a 'personal faith'. On the other hand, the representatives of the radical Reformation were arguing that one might not baptize infants at all, since these are not capable of a decision grounded in reason. Luther countered this by pointing to the questionableness of human reason and decision. He argues that often those who claim to believe do not believe at all, and those who do not believe are often believers most of all, and that human reason (and thus also the human will) is the least appropriate organ for making a decision in faith.

Over against his two opponents Luther formulated the *fides infantium*, by claiming that there was this faith in children to which Jesus himself had referred. Indeed he focusses on it by stating that the small child has the paradoxical capacity of being particularly receptive to faith because it is not yet occupied with other things.[1] 'Baptism does not make my faith, baptism receives my faith.' In a later work he goes even further: the unbaptized children whom according to the Gospel of Matthew Herod had killed in order to destroy the one child by whom he felt threatened are still called 'holy children . . . which would not be possible without the spirit and faith'. Here faith takes on a universal dimension as a basic anthropological constant. Now are these simply assertions in the framework of learned discussions about the sacrament of baptism? No. Rather, they are observations of children and recollections of his own childhood, which Luther not only never forgot but which he saw as the cause of essential later developments. That becomes particularly vivid in the sacred art inspired by him.

Who learns from whom? An exaggeration?

At the time of the Reformation a new motif entered traditional icono-
graphy[2] in Luther's circles, the image of the blessing of the children
according to Matt. 19. 13–16. Lukas Cranach depicts the scene with adult
men, looking morose, standing on the left side of the picture (!), seeking to
ward off the throng of mothers and children. In Luther's view they
embody the groups of those who according to the views of Rome and the
Radical Reformation do not acknowledge that children have any faith of
their own, but have to be instructed. However, the children are completely
orientated on their relationship with Jesus, and he is directly concerned
with them in the immediate encounter of faith. The title page of the
Deutsche Bibel is even clearer. Right up at the top sits a wise old man,
modelled on Dürer's Jerome. He is surrounded by small children with
wings, who are pointing with their fingers to a certain passage in scripture.
This must be the so-called 'gospel of the children' in which they are
instructing him (!) by directing the attention of the church's teacher to
themselves, to the children. At the side of the page scripture is being
brought down by winged children to profane children. These eagerly
accept the gospel. On the bottom margin of the picture there are once again
small children, zealously reading the Bible.

But how did Luther come to discover *fides infantium* and to attach so
much importance to it? There are impressive passages, above all in the
Table Talk, which show how much Luther observed his children,
behaviour quite extraordinary for his time. He studied them and found in
them attitudes which he failed to find in adults and which he commended
to adults, e.g. composure in the face of death. He similarly advised his
learned colleagues to study what faith is from children. His empathy was
based on his own memories. He recalled his early life history and faith and
used it more than almost any other theologian when he reported, usually in
quite a shattering way, the notion of God that was handed down to him as a
child by adults, and how far this God has been from being a forgiving God.
'I did not know the Christ child,' he had to recall.

The Christ child was kept from him, and instead he was presented with
the judge, who still drove him to despair in adult years. Only later could he
arrive at the basic image of a supportive and gracious God from another
experience, also at an early age, and add to it the image of the judge. Then
he could write: 'The Christ child hangs on the Virgin's tits.' He
rediscovered such images and his own baptism in later events of inner
tribulation and repeated them emotionally, thus finding part of the *fides*

infantium which was alive in him but which had been buried under adult indoctrination. We must see this high estimation of the child and its faith against the background of the time to recognize what a novelty it was that Luther was ready to learn from children about faith, not only in practice, but also in the theoretical development of his concept of faith. 'God must hew great chips from us to make us such children and little fools.' Here Luther is not idealizing childhood; on the contrary, it is precisely his harsh experiences then which enable him to empathize with small children. For him personally this meant finding his way back to his origins through the distortions and caricatures of faith by adults.

After his death, Luther's thoughts on the *fides infantium* were either not noted, were dismissed as incidental, or repudiated in principle.[3] Instead of this, various authors worked out developmental models of *fides* which showed the stages needed to move from infantile notions to a 'mature' faith. The child's faith then appears as an immature preliminary stage which has to be overcome.[4]

Faith

It was Freud's brilliant discovery that access to the inner life of men and women and its basic elements should be sought in early childhood, at the beginning. Here in early human experiences he also found the catalysts and conditions for later damage, defects and pathologies. This gave rise to the theory of neuroses and developmental psychology, both of which are still the subject of intensive psycho-analytical research and are of great importance for 'pastoral care'. It is above all human relations to others (so-called objects) and oneself which are formed against the background of earlier experiences with basic conflicts (Scharfenberg 1994). Thought and feeling, affects and attitudes, possibilities of fulfilment but also serious psychological blocks, seem largely to be shaped by the experience of interaction between the small child and the nearest person to whom it relates. Faith is also interaction, so it is indispensable for church pastoral care to be concerned with the inner world and its formation. Of course pastoral care is always done intuitively; however, we see today that intuition and training are not in conflict but condition each other.

Pastoral care has to do with faith. But where does faith appear in the concept of psychology? For a long time the word was completely avoided, as it seemed to have been defined and monopolized in church practice and often even emerged in a neurotic way in the psychological world.[5] But faith is an everyday term and has been taken over from everyday life. So the concept cannot be eliminated. On the contrary. We found a first cautious approach with Erikson: 'faith' was described as the trusting attitude of the very young (and very old) to life generally, caught between the poles of mistrust and trust. Michael Eigen then devoted his two notable articles to the dimension of faith in more recent psychoanalytic approaches to the first months and years of life made by researchers like Wilfred Bion, J. Lacan and Donald Winnicott. In so doing he pointed to a 'way of experiencing which is undertaken with one's whole being, all out, with all one's heart, with one's soul, and with all one's might' (Eigen 1981).

Faith is concerned with truth, the whole truth. It has something to do with myself and concerns the whole of me, not just my knowledge, but all my insights. A deep link between personality and emotionality which is characteristic of truth as a whole is still expressed in the Old Testament: Adam knew his wife Eve. For psychologists like Bion and his school this is a criterion in the situation of psychoanalysis: truth has to do with me and is emotional.

Truth is always a discovery (revelation). From such a recognition there is a way to knowledge, from truth to knowledge, but never vice versa. On the contrary, analysis (and the pastoral situation?) is concerned specifically with releasing former knowledge, with forgetting: not already providing directions for knowledge but being open to the emerging truth. The approach to truth is not knowledge, but faith. Faith is a matter of encounter, being, and not knowing. 'One cannot know truth, one must be it' (Bion 1977). In this psychoanalytical personal sense, 'science', 'knowledge' has something to do with a presuppositionless attitude. For truth truly to be experienced there is a need for perception and attention. 'Attempting to control where the truth seeks to lead us does not mean putting ourselves above the truth and thus partly excluding its possibly reorientating effects' (Eigen 1981, 353). In non-analytic language one could perhaps say that truth discloses the meaning of a situation: the subject creates meaning. It is then no longer a matter of right or wrong but of something deeper, something like a reorientation experienced by the knowing subject. The Johannine Jesus would say 'I am the truth' (John 14.6) or 'The truth will make you free' (John 8.32). It is striking that the same context mentions anxiety. In fact pure receptivity, an openness to what seeks to show itself, is something that causes anxiety. And holding on to memories and purposes is the defence against complete exposure. Here the attitude of adults in an analytical situation corresponds to that of the small child: if learning means change, the small child is constantly exposed to the restructuring of its knowledge and also the apparatus by which it knows. What it perceives are primarily physical sensations – disordered, chaotic, causing anxiety. Psychological birth has to do with experiencing this catastrophe, and only through it is new order and thought possible. And real encounter with truth is structurally a new birth (John 3.3). 'Can an adult be reborn?', asks Nicodemus. Bion says that it is an artificial attitude to leave aside all security and expose oneself to the encounter. So encounter with truth can cause anxiety and provoke defensiveness. 'Over and over the baby dies and is reborn' (Eigen 1985, 329). Thus the adult subject who encounters the truth experiences rebirth. This can happen on the basis of a fundamental sense of continuity which does not spare us tribulation and catastrophe, but even makes it an ingredient of faith. We do not completely lose ourselves, because of a capacity for detachment. Step by step the baby develops the capacity to distinguish between being and experiencing. Only in people who lack this capacity, who are trapped in mental confusion, is the whole of inner being a catastrophe. We others have the possibility to distinguish between 'I experience catastrophe' and 'I am catastrophe', a capacity which develops early in the psychological life of children.

Bion's ideas, which have been reproduced here very briefly, become more comprehensible if one adopts his basic model of inner life. Here too he begins from earliest childhood. He describes how for a long time the small child cannot assimilate even for perception and thought the sensations which impinge upon it. Rather, these are time and again fragile psychological units which first of all are experienced and expressed above all physically. The child still does not 'know' what it is experiencing. It is not detached; it is exposed to its own feelings and only slowly constructs the apparatus which enables it to realize the experience and fit it into its thoughts. As we can observe, this time is accompanied by violent inner storms. The child needs its mother, who accepts what the child gives of itself in the attitude of a child; she can think and inwardly assimilate what she accepts. This is returned to the child in a tolerable form, in language or in a pre-linguistic way, in tones or attitudes which the child can perceive again. This process, which from an external perspective may be called comforting, is the 'work' of the mother, and serves as a 'container' in which something is put to be processed and from which it can then be returned. The process can be seen as analogous to digestion. The aim of early development is not just to collect assimilable experiences but to form a container with the help of which the growing person can bring his or her impressions to the level of thought. It now seems to me that this model gives a very impressive description of what faith can be: the way of experiencing and assimilating experiences in their full claim to truth. Here we are back at Eigen's initial definition. The model ('projective identification') also gives us an idea of how the pastoral situation, prayer and the church institution can be understood: as a vessel in which something can originate and in which the inner world of a person can be restored.

This brief and very selective report on psychoanalytical research is not just meant to indicate that there is such a thing as *fides*, faith – as something very elemental; it is also meant to show that the earliest fortunes of this basic element are experienced at a very early age, and how they happen, how these fortunes quite essentially determine how we perceive, i.e. inwardly create, the world, ourselves and our personal encounter. This 'inner world' as it is understood by psychoanalysis is the place of relationship and faith, the stage on which the 'theatre of the soul' (McDougall 1992) is played out. Here psychoanalysis refers in particular to the significance of the early and earliest environment present in the first reference person, the mother.

Psychoanalysis shows the dependence, indeed the helplessness, of human beings in the face of their early environment and the powers of their own psyche, and describes particularly clearly the threats and breaks which must be integrated from the first day on. Faith is not then misunderstood as a glad possession but as a process of end and beginning, of no and yes, of death and rebirth. It so to speak includes unbelief. It need not be instilled or even aroused; what it needs is an appropriate environment for coping with damage and with constant shaking. It is something given; theologians speak of a gift. It needs symbols for expressing inner experience and communicating it (Scharfenberg 1994).

This impressive picture of the infant and its *fides* has recently again been disturbed by results from research into infants. This may be widely noted in the next few years. The picture of the infant as a being exposed only to the pleasure principle and visited by inner storms is being shattered. The new image of the small child is called 'competence'.

The competent baby

In a large series of investigations, experiments have shown how active the human child already is in the first days, weeks and months of its life. It has a great arsenal of capabilities which are important for life and a particularly important property of its own: an active interest in its environment, its curiosity. A picture is coming into being of the infant as a 'researcher' into itself, its body and also the 'objects' in its environment. What is particularly marked is the need for contingency, i.e. the experience of connections. There are true moments of happiness when an infant discovers that an action of its own has a consequence in its environment, when for example it realizes that it can move a mobile or direct a projector by certain sucking movements on a dummy. This experience of its own effects is special in relation to a living counterpart, i.e. to its mother. Delight in bringing something about is a central motivation of the small child. It also remains central for the whole of later life and adult faith. This is also true in relation to God, as Jesus' provocative statements say: 'Ask and it will be given to you, knock and it will be opened to you' (Matt. 7.7). Faith can be severely threatened if the person concerned has to experience that his or her existence has no effect.

We see in the baby above all its helplessness and dependence. But precisely in this state it is capable of directing its mother and other adults and bending them to its needs. The cry is not only a signal of need or helplessness but also an expression of a power over adults who have to hear it and act. Here the *fides infantium* takes on a new characteristic: it is a form of competence and control of the world which is present from the first day on and is very elementary. The baby has interests, has power and curiosity. It seeks connections and can be amazed at surprises. It has intentionality, a fundamental 'being directed towards' which the theologian Paul Tillich describes as a basic structure of faith. It is closely involved in the emergence of an inner world, the long process of the formation of representations and symbolizations, i.e. those structures, expectations, experiences, ideas which determine us, mostly without our being aware of it.

The *fides infantium* can also be irritated. This becomes clear from one of the best known and at the same time experiments of researches into babies, the so-called still-face situation, which I reproduce here in abbreviated form.[9] The mother is asked to arrange to be with her baby as they would normally be at home. She is to play for three minutes and then leave the room. After three minutes she is to return to the room and then spend another three minutes with the child, but without taking the slightest notice of it, not reacting to the child or influencing it in any way. The behaviour of mother and baby is recorded on two video-cameras:

A girl of three months, one of hundreds with whom this experiment was tried, plays with her fingers when her mother leaves the room. When the mother returns, she stops playing and makes eye contact with a smile. As instructed, her mother displays a mask-like unmoved expression. The baby quickly looks away with a serious face. After twenty seconds she looks the mother in the face again with raised eyebrows and eyes wide open, and stretches out her arms – hardly perceptibly towards the mother. No reaction from the mother. The baby looks at her hands, pulls at her fingers for about eight seconds and then looks at the mother again questioningly. In the meantime she has to yawn and her head goes back. Again the child pulls at her fingers. Her body does not move; there is a frightened arm movement, a short look at her mother's face. The arms move back. The corners of her mouth drop and her eyes go small. She turns her head to the side, looks at the mother from there, plays with her fingers, stretches her legs towards her mother and then immediately draws them back. She bends in the chair, almost falls over, and presses her chin on her shoulder, but looks at her mother with lowered chin. She keeps in this position for more than a minute, looking towards the mother between times. She pulls a face, becomes more serious, wrinkles her eyebrows. Finally the baby draws right into itself, bends her body forward and lets her head drop. She now no longer looks at her mother, just sucks her finger. She gives a defeated, helpless and quite withdrawn impression. When her mother goes the baby half looks up and gazes in her direction. The baby's melancholy expression and bowed attitude remain unchanged.

The reactions of the small child show a serious inner crisis of the kind that we keep experiencing in our childhood – without any experiments being arranged. In its reactions and the results of withdrawal and melancholy down to the smallest detail, it shows the features of the crisis of faith of an adult.

Various elements of faith become clear in this experiment:

Reciprocity: from the first moment of its life the child depends on an encounter, a reciprocal relationship. This is an essential characteristic of faith, especially in the Christian sphere.

Dependence on contingencies: there are innate and acquired sequences of expectation in the form of if-then. If the expectation is confirmed, a feeling of happiness ensues. If it is disappointed, then this can first be used for new learning. Only if the contingency shatters does withdrawal follow as protection from the perception of meaningless.

Pleasure in achieving something. The small child has an enormous range of appelative and reparative capacities in its *fides*, and only if these have no change does it sink into unmourning melancholia.

The face is at the same time the expression of what is going on within and a means of communication and attention, and as such is vitally important.

These few examples must be enough to sketch out the fascinating area of research into infants. The 'competent baby' represents a necessary counterpart to the helpless child subject to its drives, which has been accepted hitherto and has determined nurture. However, competence fits better into the feeling of our time and it must be noted that an understanding of faith as competence alone similarly must produce a one-sided picture, a caricature of humanity. The experiments of those who research into babies can cover only those activities in which a child is relatively balanced and awake. They cannot expose the child to any frustrations. The still-face situation is itself on the borderline of what is ethically defensible. So an important part of the early experience of children escapes even researchers into babies. Their results tend towards an idealization and functionalization of the baby and do not cover those areas with which psychoanalysis in particular grapples. Thus the process of the *fides infantium* will also have to be put between two poles, the experience of exposure, helplessness and tribulation and the experience of competence and learning.

I end with a question. What are the consequences for the action of the church and theological doctrine of the insight that faith is to be regarded not only in theory but in experience as a gift, that even churches and their officers can only serve a faith which is already present, can never administer or produce it, but can disturb or corrupt it?

Translated by John Bowden

A select bibliography

1. *Theological authors*: Augustine, *Confessions*; Martin Luther, *Works*; Joachim Scharfenberg, *Einführung in die Pastoralpsychologie*, Stuttgart 1994; Klaus Winkler, *Werden wie die Kinder*, Mainz 1992.

2. *Psychoanalytical authors*: Wilfred Bion, *Learning from Experience*, London 1984; id., *Attention and Interpretation*, London 1970; Michael Eigen, 'The Area of Faith in Winnicott, Lacan and Bion', *International Journal of Psychoanalysis* 1981; id., 'Towards Bion's Starting Point: Between Catastrophe and Faith', ibid., 1985; E. H. Erikson, *Life-Cycle Completed: A Review*, New York 1993; Wolfgang Loch, *Deutungskunst*, Tübingen 1993; Donald Winnicott, *Playing and Reality*, London 1971.

3. *Research into small children*: B. Brazelton and B. Cramer, *Die frühe Bindung*, Munich 1975; Daniel Stern, *Diary of a Baby*, London 1991; id., *Mother and Child. The First Relationship*, London 1993; Martin Dornes, *Der kompetente Säugling*, Frankfurt 1993.

Notes

1. *Parvulus est capacior, id est patentior, nullis rebus implicatus. Commentary on Romans.*

2. For what follows, cf. Werner Hofmann, *Luther und die Folgen für die Kunst*, Munich 1983.

3. Karl Barth is said to have remarked that this was an invention of theologians to rescue infant baptism (which he did not accept) and the established-type church arising from it.

4. One example is Klaus Thomans, in *Handbuch der Neurosenlehre und Psychotherapie*, vol. 5, Munich 1961.

5. Oskar Pfister, the Zurich pastor and friend of Freud, who claimed a special right for faith from an early stage, was an exception here, cf. Eckhart Nase, *Oskar Pfisters Analytische Seelsorge*, Berlin 1993.

6. Described e.g. in Brazelton and Cramer, 123ff.

Solidarity between the Generations

Ursula Peukert

I The conditions in which children grow up

The need for children to be brought up arises out of what S. Bernfeld has called 'the fact of development', namely that human beings require a long-drawn out process of developing physical and psychological capacities if they are to be able to survive. The care which allows the rising generation to flourish in its helplessness safeguards its physical birth and, from the perspective of evolution, the preservation of the species. However, with human beings, along with physical birth there arises the task of helping individuals towards 'cultural birth'. For the change of generations also involves the transmission of forms of life which have grown up in history and the communication of the knowledge and skill which makes young people capable of being active in a particular society and culture. It is this responsibility for the well-being of the next generation, what E. H. Erikson called the original 'sense of generativity', that creates the conditions for survival at the human level.

However, it seems that such a relationship between the generations can no longer be taken for granted. A wide-ranging discussion has developed over the question whether the processes which aim to form and bring up young people are not in danger, and whether society's power of socialization generally has not decreased with the accelerating process of modernization (cf. e.g. Elkind 1994; Heitmeyer 1994; H. Peukert 1992; Coleman 1982). There is much to suggest that such fears are justified. It is becoming increasingly clear that the conditions in which children grow up are governed not only by the behaviour of individuals but more deeply and more lastingly by shared political and economic decisions. The changes which have been set in motion affect the very foundations of society and consequently are also changing the basic presuppositions of upbringing.

In the highly industrialized countries certain aspects of human practice like economics, politics and culture have become independent sub-systems. All spheres of life are covered by their rational planning, which is concerned to achieve efficiency and increased effectiveness; under their influence traditional forms of social life which safeguard identity are losing validity, becoming intrinsically contradictory, and are gradually dissolving. Individuals have to work out an orientation for themselves. The loss of security in one's own orientation which individualization necessarily brings is experienced to a heightened degree through a number of concurrent processes. First, migratory movements produce *de facto* multi-cultural societies in which confrontation with alien traditions is unavoidable. Secondly, unemployment and impoverishment as mass phenomena threaten not only material but also psycho-social security.

The conditions in which children grow up have changed fundamentally with these general trends in society. First the trends have led to a fundamental change in the family. In the process of the loss of tradition, which primarily shows itself as social disintegration, new cultural patterns of interpretation of the social role of the woman, of partnership and parenthood are gradually emerging. As these new patterns are in principle all centred on equal rights and self-determination, the task of integrating them into unitary form of life is becoming more demanding, and to a considerable degree depends on the capacity and readiness of all concerned to reflect and arrive at a consensus. Although the 'trend towards the late child' is diminishing the chronological status of the family phase when adults plan their lives, the demands on parenthood are increasing with the rise of a new child-centred family model. At the same time children are increasingly felt to be a burden and a disadvantage in the attempt to assert oneself in the marketplace of work. Insights into their need for protection and concern for their needs seem to be declining. In the 'post-modern family' it is the adults who claim all the freedom to decide how they are to fulfil themselves – at the expense of the children (Elkind 1994).

These intrinsically contradictory tendencies are making the network of family relationships more fragile – while at the same time expectations of its contribution towards safeguarding identity are increasing. This is shown by the rising number of alternative forms of family like step-families and one-parent families, and also the increase in conspicuous forms of behaviour, of neglect, aggression and stress-related illness among children. The problems are intensified by processes of impoverishment, by which families with children in the rich industrialized countries are disproportionately affected. The imperatives of an economic and bureaucratic rationality which are increasingly penetrating all spheres of life threaten to disturb or even destroy the very process of mutual understanding which first produced the new forms of family life and reliable relationships which are a necessary presupposition for bringing up children and at the same time could stabilize them. Obviously the complex task of constructing new forms of life – necessitated by social developments and at the same time endangered by them – cannot be foisted on the family alone. In the end that would mean privatizing problems caused by society and making permanent the 'cultural heedlessness' of society (Kaufmann 1990).

The so-called developing countries are more affected by these tendencies which are developing in industrial countries, and much more harshly, though the causes there are different. Not only have their social traditions been disturbed or even destroyed by colonization and ongoing exploitation by the industrial countries, but in the global economic competition whole societies are being impoverished and thus prevented from developing authentic forms of life against the background of their own cultural heritage. Instead of this, the fragmented forms of life of the industrial countries are being imposed on them, and it is questionable whether such forms can secure humane social life in the future. In this situation children, the next generation, no longer represent social wealth, but increased misery and distress. For the majority of children in Third World countries, despite all the efforts that have been made, there is no *a priori* guarantee either of the possibility of physical survival or of opportunities for intellectual development and psychological well-being (Boehnke/Reddy 1993, 177).

In these conditions, what is the meaning of solidarity between the generations and above all solidarity with the next generation – a solidarity which not only appeals to individual responsibility but also entails structural consequences?

II Development and upbringing as a process of reaching an understanding

The question how development and upbringing can be appropriately understood at all can be answered only when the way in which the child appropriates reality and gradually becomes an independent autonomous person who can take part in human communication has been explained in principle. This has been discussed for a long time and is a matter of controversy. Some authorities have made the process of maturing exclusively responsible for this development and have thought that the child simply had to be given enough room and time. Others have thought that they could explain the attainment of thought, speech and social capabilities solely from learning processes conditioned by the environment and have focussed on the instruction of the child to further its development.

However, the 'cultural birth of the human being' is clearly a more complex process. It was Jean Piaget (cf. e.g. Piaget 1950) who pointed out that the child has an active and creative involvement in its environment. It has to 'invent' the world of objects and its relationship to itself and others in its actions, as it were by itself. This 'construction of reality' arises from the child's increasing capacity to discover the environment with all its senses. By dealing with objects it learns to construct an ordered space and to perceive itself as an agent in this space, i.e. as someone who can purposefully achieve certain effects through actions. This activity gives rise to a unitary and structured world which the child can survey, which has a clear meaning and within which individual actions and objects gain significance. So one can understand the whole process of development as 'creating significance and meaning' (Kegan 1982).

However, this 'practical intelligence' of the child and the construction of reality which corresponds to it is primarily dependent on the child's immediate action and therefore limited. Coping with the fundamental regularities of action at a new stage by picturing them, then translating them into thought-processes and finally making them the objects of thought is a development which extends well into youth. The transitions to each new level of thought and action are difficult, because each time they mean bidding farewell to a previous view of the world and a previous understanding of the self.

But even Piaget's concept of development as the construction and reconstruction of reality in stages cannot in itself cover the complexity of the process of development. Piaget described the small child as 'egocentric'. By this he did not mean a moral weakness in the child, but rather wanted to characterize a peculiarity of its thought: as long as its thought is tied to perception, the child perceives only parts of a problem without relating them; this deficiency also limits its social capacities, so that it does not succeed in integrating the standpoint of the other into its own action. Now if we not only analyse what the child says about its behaviour but – unlike Piaget – observe it directly in dealings with those around it in familiar situations, a different picture arises. Then the child proves to be a quite competent conversation partner. Human ethology has been able to show that in the very first months of life, in the exchange of direct contact, the child has already mastered the essential rules of conduct: making contact, noting the changing roles of speaker and listener, reacting appropriately to the contributions of the other and finally ending the 'conversation' or avoiding it altogether (Stern 1977). Playing with objects, which presupposes motor skills, is incorporated into this direct mutuality later, towards the end of the first year of life. Thus the complete structure of communication is already developed at this early stage: being able to co-operate with others by integrating one's own purposes and those of others into a common goal and realizing them in shared activity. It has been claimed, probably rightly, that the whole further development of the child 'merely' consists in working out this capacity for reciprocity and co-operation over things, above all by catching up with language, developing new and more numerous partners and finally also reflecting on the structure of this interaction.

The foundation on which human capacities first come into being is thus the fragile medium of social interaction itself. Development, the construction of reality, becomes clear as a social, interactive process in which both the adult and the child are involved, as a shared construction, as 'co-construction' (Youniss 1994). But even if the child is involved from the beginning, the adult needs to do certain things first so that the dialogue can unfold and develop: there is a need for sensitivity to the intentions of the child and readiness to take them up and thus recognize it as a partner. The child 'recognizes' itself only in its reflection: if the adult accepts what is offered by the child and presents it to the child by way of imitation, if the adult surprises the child with unknown new things and thus carefully challenges its capacities.

However, it would be a mistake to think that these preliminary actions by the adult were limited to maintaining the private sphere of reciprocity between it and the child. Rather, adults represent for the child a historical world which is communicated and interpreted by language, a form of life which is handed down by culture – and research into learning to talk above all has drawn attention to this. With the first word adults disclose to the child a public world of shared meaning (Bruner 1983). The step into language presupposes shared contexts of action which form the horizon for mutual understanding and first make individual objects accessible for naming. So language is initially always related to situations, indeed it is itself communicative action in situations. The child, by learning to represent to itself and others through the medium of speech the events and actions which are involved in situations, depicting areas of free play for interpretation and action and thus also laying claim to them, grows into a social form of life and acquires an understanding of itself, i.e. its own identity, and differentiated capacities for dealing with objects, with persons and its own inner impulses: in other words cognitive, social and linguistic competences. So development as a creative, interactive process is also what J. S. Bruner has called a process of 'culture creation', a creative process in which culture keeps coming into being anew.

What can be a more precise meaning of upbringing against this background? Recent research presents the child as a being who from the beginning has an active and creative concern along with others to produce meaning; it therefore seeks reciprocity and permanent communication and will get involved in this (Dunn 1988). Here we have what could be called the 'morality' of the child. It is a morality which receives its inner orientation from a solidarity with adults – though of course at first it is quite unreflected and naive. What from the standpoint of the observer can seem to be adaptation and subordination to the perspective of adults, indeed, as L. Kohlberg puts it, as a primitive orientation on obedience and punishment, can from the child's perspective be understood as the often already desperate attempt to make connections and feel at one with the beloved adult.

It is not least the achievement of psychoanalysis that this dependence makes the child itself highly vulnerable. For it cannot direct its actions reflectively, but only decide who it wants to be by going straight to the other. Its action is its description of itself and the way in which it understands itself. The necessary step in learning consists in the child being able to detach itself from this 'bound identity' (U. Peukert 1985) by attaining a first form of reflecting on itself, by being able to give information about its own actions and thus gain distance.

III Solidarity between the generations as a postulate for interaction in upbringing

How can the task of the adult be defined more precisely? Evidently it does not just consist of individual pedagogical interventions but rather of sharing with the child the building of a common world. This calls for the capacity to perceive the different way in which the child constructs reality, and to look at and examine one's own understanding of reality from its perspective. Such mobility and capacity to learn is presupposed in our dealings with other people, but to a heightened degree it is part of the competence which enables teaching to be done. As the development and elementary learning of the child is extremely prone to disruption, adults have an obligation to develop and maintain a framework of communication in which they can be protected and furthered.

This creates a situation of communication which since Martin Buber has been called 'paradoxical'. On the one hand it is a matter of recognizing the child in what it does itself and thus from the beginning as a person in its own right, a capacity which the child first has to learn. On the other hand the adult must constantly be the child's representative and act in anticipation of its future development. The adult then runs the risk of either manipulating the child in accordance with his or her own unfulfilled wishes or projections or exposing it directly to the pressure of social expectations.

Because concrete possibilities of self-development open up to the child only through the preliminary interpretation of the adult, which puts its action in the wider context of a defined social world, the child can fail to find itself. It is exposed to the superior power of the partner in the interaction and forced to adapt. The relationship between child and adult is so precarious because the adult is dominant, equipped with an advantage of knowledge and ability which the child cannot catch up with, and because the adult must bring into a relationship with the child not only his or her possibilities, but also his or her limitations and hurts. However, if the adult attempts to reflect on this asymmetry with the child and to change it into an 'inter-generational reciprocity', the child is recognized as a partner on an equal footing and thus the communicative presupposition is created for a development in which the child can learn for its part to recognize others as others (cf. U. Peukert 1979). Only a solidarity with the next generation which has this structure opens up the possibility of growing into humane forms of social life and appropriating them.

IV Respect for the next generation

Recent research has increasingly emphasized that the interaction in a group of children is just as important as interaction with adults (Krappmann/Peukert 1995), for here the child cannot rely on the interpretative contributions of adults but must itself make the framework of communication. Elementary and necessary processes of formation take place in a group of children, without which the capacities which the competent and responsible adult needs cannot completely be attained. These are social, but also cognitive and moral capacities, in the reciprocal interlocking which children acquire in dealings with one another. In arguing over plans for play a child first learns what it means to find a partner and enthuse the partner over its own idea without being snubbed; it learns how one arrives at a shared understanding of a situation, how conflicts can be solved constructively without endangering the togetherness; and in so doing it learns how to make compromises without betraying itself and others. Children learn to argue in order to work out what is and what is not to be allowed. They learn the meaning of social rules and how things can be done fairly and justly. What children increasingly work out together and at a primary school age ultimately quite without the help of adults – often in hard disputes – are both the presuppositions for developing and maintaining relations with other people and the presuppositions for co-operation. In this way they discover the foundations for human society as it were all over again and work out the basis of all culture. It is then no exaggeration to speak of the social world of children as a 'children's culture' (Krappmann 1993). The group is the place where children submit themselves to those processes of education from which an identity orientated on justice, trust and solidarity and a competence to act humanely arises – and that not as a task imposed from outside but out of the inner need to organize one's life with and among others.

Adults also have an important function to play in securing the success of these autonomous processes of formation. First of all they must accept that groups of children are their own authority for socialization and formation and fulfil roles which they themselves cannot perceive. And this is already true of small children. But adults must also realize that their help and support are not simply superfluous. Constructivist developmental psychology which starts from the child's own creative activity encourages an understanding of education which promises the child self-determination and autonomy, precisely by recognizing its own way of dealing with reality. Now respect for the person of a child does not mean paradoxically expecting too much of it and endangering its development by excessive demands. The real experiment of the 'street children' shows vividly the consequences of a 'high speed existence' which asks too much and is too quickly burdened with adult tasks.

It is vital for adults to adapt their control and support to the state of children's development, because not only a lack of help but also too much help can endanger the social world of children. Here 'solidarity between the generations' is realized in allowing children their own responsibility and independence without abandoning concern for their well-being. In bidding farewell to the functions of parent and changing the adult-child relationship into a relationship in which both partners finally give each other autonomy and can live autonomously, the adult is also required to recognize the finitude of his or her own human existence.

V Solidarity between the generations as a political task

Upbringing as the construction of a world together with a new generation is a process of original creativity and elementary productivity: it is a creative event from which a humane culture keeps arising anew. Responsibility for the next generation is the paradigm for a human responsibility which extends beyond one's own life-span and one's own death. But to individualize this responsibility does not go far enough. The influences in modern society cannot be limited to face-to-face interaction; they are a web of the consequences and fall-out of actions which in turn have an effect on everyday life. In present-day societies upbringing is also a prime example of the 'dialectic of modernization'. Functional rationalization in all social spheres leads to the direct interaction of alien structures being overlaid, 'colonized', as Habermas puts it. Sociologists therefore diagnose a dissolution of social resources, and economists in particular state that the traditional authorities of socialization no longer prepare as it were free of charge the social qualifications without which a society cannot function, like the capacity to negotiated shared rules, to work together in a team, to be stable under pressure and reliable in agreements. Whereas on the one hand social erosion is increasing, on the other the need to get on and understand one another in a global network of communication is increasing. But understanding and solidarity cannot be produced technically. If our societies are to continue to function, people in them must not just function, but must assume responsibility for living together in a more comprehensive sense, in their awareness and the orientation of their actions.

So the relationship between generations is not just a relationship between individuals. If the process of education always also involves the construction of a new world and thus the anticipation of changed structures of communication, then this process can only be understood as one of learning between generations which has social dimensions and is orientated on the future. The quest for new humane forms of life may not therefore be loaded on children and families alone; the utopia of human society without alienation must not be sought only in the new beginning of the growing-up of children. Solidarity between the generations must therefore be understood in two ways, on the one hand as an attitude of adults which enters into direct interaction with children, and on the other as the concern of the generation now living and thus society as a whole for the conditions which make living towards the future possible and which must be introduced in shared binding political decisions. Only a culture of mutuality and solidarity which embraces family and community can provide the necessary framework for the processes of education on which societies in all their dimensions are dependent. The horizon against which a theory of upbringing must be developed is the question how forms of living in solidarity can be produced which are not destructive and in which each person can be recognized as a subject and recognize others as subjects.

Translated by John Bowden

Bibliography

K. Boehnke and N. Y. Reddy, 'Kindheit in Armutsgesellschaften', in *Handbuch der Kindheitsforschung*, ed. M. Markefka and B. Nauck, Neuwied 1993, 177–89.

J. S. Bruner, *Child's Talk: Learning to Use Language*, New York and London 1983.

J. S. Coleman, *The Asymmetric Society*, Syracuse 1982.

J. Dunn, *The Beginnings of Social Understanding*, Oxford 1988.

D. Elkind, *Ties that Stress: The New Family Imbalance*, Cambridge, Mass. and London 1994.

W. Heitmeyer (ed.), *Das Gewalt-Dilemma*, Frankfurt am Main 1994.

F. X. Kaufmann, *Zukunft der Familie*, Munich 1990.

R. Kegan, *The Evolving Self. Problem and Process in Human Development*, Cambridge, Mass. 1982.

L. Krappmann, 'Kinderkultur als institutionalisierte Entwicklungsaufgabe', in *Handbuch der Kindheitsforschung*, ed. M. Markefka and B. Nauck, Neuwied 1993, 365–76.

L. Krappmann and U. Peukert (eds), *Altersgemischte Gruppen in Kindertagesstätten. Reflexionen und Praxisberichte zu einer neuen Betreuungsform*, Freiburg im Breisgau 1995.

J. Piaget, *The Psychology of Intelligence*, London 1950.

U. Peukert, 'Die Erziehungswissenschaft der Moderne und die Herausforderungen der Gegenwart', *Zeitschrift für Pädagogie*, Beiheft 19, 1992, 113–27.

U. Peukert, 'Identitätsentwicklung', in J. Zimmer (ed.), *Erziehung in früher Kindheit*, Enzyklopädie Erziehungswissenschaft 6, Stuttgart 1985, 326–8.

U. Peukert, *Interaktive Kompetenz und Identitat*, Düsseldorf 1979.

D. Stern, *The First Relationship. Infant and Mother*, London 1977.

J. Youniss, *Soziale Konstruktion und psychische Entwicklung*, Frankfurt am Main 1994.

III · Practical Consequences

The Church as an Advocate of Children

Georg Sporschill

'Moreover your little ones, who you said would become a prey, and your children, who this day have no knowledge of good or evil, shall go in there, and to them I will give it' (Deut. 1.39). It is for their sake – not for the sake of the fathers or the great prophetic figures, but for the sake of the children – that God gives the Torah, his loving word, to the people of Israel. The present generation is destined to wander through the wilderness, suffering tribulations, burdens, anxieties and conflicts. Certainly the Israelites must listen, but they are all doomed to leave their bodies in the wilderness. However, they have this promise: their way was not in vain. They have the experience that their way was not only long but also rich. It was always directed towards the next generation, and that means the children.

Jesus takes up this tradition when he commands, 'Suffer the little children to come to me and forbid them not, for theirs is the kingdom of heaven' (Matt. 19.14). He blessed the children. He told adults to learn from children, to become like them, because there is no other way into the kingdom of heaven. 'Unless you convert and become like children, you cannot enter into the kingdom of heaven' (Matt. 18.3). Here Jesus is not inviting children to become childish but to learn from the child immediacy, trust, desire, courage and joy in life.

The background to this high value attached to the child is the high view of human beings as a result of which the Bible brands any exploitation and any abuse of individuals as betrayal of the will of God, who has created human beings in his image. So God himself removes people from the authority of others: he is the only authority over them. In this way earthly authority is relativized and subjected to God's rules. God himself protects people by directing any authority by his own. God takes the side of the weak and especially children: 'He has scattered the proud in the imagination of their hearts; he has put down the mighty from their thrones, and exalted those of low degree' (Luke 1.51f.). This orientation can be seen most clearly in the child, since the child needs the authority of parents and society to be able to live and develop. At the same time this marvellous being, the child, is protected from human authority, because God makes the rules for all authority.

In dealing with children there come days when a generation proves itself or fails them because in the child the weakness inherent in any human being lies open to authority and social systems. The following four stories about my encounters with children in Vienna and Bucharest are to be seen against this background.

At Bucharest station

In 1991 I came to Bucharest on behalf of Caritas to start a project for street children. First I and my colleagues went to the station, where we were soon surrounded by curious, dirty young figures who were drug addicts, sick and aggressive. It was a difficult, disturbing, dangerous situation which filled me with anxiety. It was only because I had previously spent ten years in a house with homeless young people out of prison who were drug addicts that I was able to stand firm and remain there, despite the aggression shown to us by the children. This aggression was basically a test. Are they tourists like the others? Can we play with them? What are we going to get from them? What do they want? These questions determined the behaviour of the children.

Then we began to establish a small home in a ruin, a house with no windows or heating. We renovated it in the winter, and the children quickly got to know of it. The communication among them, the street network, functioned well. And they thronged in on us day and night, indeed once even attacked us in the night, because they all wanted to get into the house – and because they wanted a trial of strength. In our idealism at first we took thirty children into our small house, far too many to create a community, order, and a peaceful atmosphere. A bitter fight began over places in the home. Finally we reduced them to twenty-five, which was a painful, chance and unjust process.

One afternoon I was standing at the door when a small boy came along. He reached just up to my waist. He said quite definitely, in an almost authoritarian way, 'I'm staying here.' I was so surprised that I quite forgot that we had just reduced the number of children, indeed had sent some away in order to survive. The small boy marched into the house, I put down a mattress and he went to sleep immediately, without even having the courtesy to speak to me. The next day he woke up, and ate and drank sullenly before we could put the questions to him that we have to put to all our children: 'Do you have parents? Where have you run away from? How long have you been on the street? What's your name?' He was very taciturn and when it came to parents he simply said, 'I have parents, but they aren't interested in me.' Then the conversation broke off. During the next days and weeks, when we again tried to take up the conversation, he would only keep repeating this one sentence, which I had never heard before, 'I have parents, but they aren't interested in me.' I supposed that he had no parents, and that as he didn't like confessing this, he used this tactic to get out of things.

The boy was then accepted into the group of twenty-five children and joined in the process which is planned for all, which attempts to bring order into the life of the children, to teach cleanliness, going to sleep at particular times, and having some manners when eating. It sought to bring out how much he had already learned at school, since he could not yet read and write. And then there was daily teaching to prepare him one day to go to a state school. This introduction into the community of our little home lasted a whole year.

One of our teachers was particularly involved in his integration. She was his friend, sister and mother all in one. After about a year had passed, he suddenly took her by the hand and said, 'Come with me to the station!' She was surprised, since usually our children don't want to go back to the station where they had once vegetated for months or years in an atmosphere of drugs, prostitution, beggars and thieves. But again he was quite definite, as was his nature. She went with him and at the station he took her into the toilets. There in the darkness a figure was crouching. He just said, 'That's my mother.' It was a tearful, touching reunion. No one knows whether he had ever gone there during that year, but one thing was clear: he had tested us for a year; it took us a whole year to build up the necessary trust and relationship to him before he could reveal himself to us and give us his secret. 'That's my mother.'

His mother lived at the station with her daughter, the sister of our small Julian, as a toilet woman. For money, the two were allowed to spend the night in a cabin with their scant possessions, to live in a place where one could not lie down but could only sleep sitting. Of course people were sick or had to become sick to bear that. After that Julian visited his mother regularly. The station is only ten minutes' walk from our house, and the boy invited teachers and friends, indeed selected them, to go with him to the station. It was as it were a great reward when he invited someone to meet his mother.

One day he found an Austrian shilling, knotted it firmly in his handkerchief and said to the person in charge of the house, 'I must go to the Austrian ambassador, because I've something important to discuss with him.' 'That's not very easy,' she said, and didn't take him very seriously. He got angry and insisted on his wish being met. When he got nowhere he said, 'Now I'll really tell you what it's about. I've a lot of money and I want to put it in a bank in Austria. I promise I'll only use the interest, just enough to feed my mother and my sister, but the money will stay there in the bank.' He had felt responsible that one day his mother and his sister should have a better life. He wanted nothing for himself, but only for his mother and sister.

I told this story once in a sermon at Christmas and in fact afterwards people gave me so much money that we were able to find a room for his mother and his sister. So although we laughed at it to begin with, his plan with the shilling worked. He took responsibility, and so gave us responsibility in a new task. The story continued: he left our home of his own accord – we encouraged him – and joined up with his mother and sister (we know nothing of his father). But after only a few days he asked to be allowed back into the home because he could not bear living with his psychologically disturbed, alcoholic mother. We took him back into the home and since then he has gone regularly to look after his family. He looks like a ten-year-old (although he is now thirteen), but he is strong. He is choosy about whom he trusts; that takes time. He has taken responsibility and maintained it, and has also survived setbacks. That is one experience with a child who took over the leadership from me in my work for the street children and showed us the way.

Children take over the leadership

Another story. Costel was one of the first children I got to know in Rumania. I met him at the North station, and because he spoke quite good English he overcame my language barriers. He told me that he spent every night in a video shop. During the day he begged enough money on the game to be able to watch films until he fell asleep and so could spend the night there. That was how he had learned English.

Costel had a very dark complexion and was lively, almost wild. That pleased me, and I took him into our house. However, there he was difficult. The staff couldn't cope with him. He was quite disordered, and wouldn't obey any rules. He kept running away and I could no longer protect him; he had to go back on the street. When I saw him again in the Metro station in which he then lived, I felt so sorry for him that I took him back: it was winter, it was cold, and he looked hungry. But the staff went on strike and declared that if he was allowed to get away with it we wouldn't have even minimal order in the house and couldn't develop community and provide training. So he was not allowed to stay. It was then a good six months until I met him again. He looked frightful, almost starving, with a very dark, drawn face and said: 'Please take me into the house, now I'll always be good.' I knew that this would be impossible for him, but he was so sincere and convincing that I took him. He had made me and the staff determined to try another experiment. This time, in fact, he did stay with us. We even succeeded in getting him to school and stopping him from smoking at least in the house, and persuaded him to fall in with the normal rhythm of life with others.

Our home in Bucharest keeps being visited by people who particularly like talking to Costel because he is the only one who can speak English and also has the gift of putting himself forward. He is then often asked, 'What is your aim in life?' Once he replied in a flash: 'One day I want to go to New York and one day I want to see Jesus.' We all thought that one day he might perhaps succeed in getting to New York, but would he ever see Jesus? A few weeks after this visit he came to us smartly dressed, with a blue tie which he had found somewhere among the things we had been given, and we reprimanded him. 'You're showing off – that's taking it a bit far!' He had already had difficulty with the other children because he was so fond of pushing himself forward. But he said, 'Why? I'm wearing the tie because I'm being baptized on Sunday.'

I didn't believe him and investigated. In fact, without my knowledge and the knowledge of the staff he had been taking religious instruction with a pastor to prepare himself for baptism because he wanted to become a Jesuit. So he had quite deliberately looked for a Catholic priest, and they are not so easy to find in Bucharest. On the great day of his baptism we were guests. The priest gave a fine sermon and said: 'You've never known a family. But now you do have a family, a community. Look round, we're your family.' After the baptism something quite unusual happened: he, the boaster, the strong one, the leader, wept bitterly. We asked him, 'Why are you crying?' He said in good English, 'I was standing in front of the living God.' Yes, he did meet Jesus, and perhaps one day if he keeps on learning he will also get to New York.

Costel proudly calls himself 'Americanul', 'the American', because he speaks English, or rather American, so well, and the other children call him that too. This explains why he wanted to get to New York one day. But he has since given up his wish because he has heard that there are also drug problems and criminality in New York. That has destroyed his dream of America. During the three or four years he has been living with us we tracked down his mother with the help of the police and went to see her. His mother looked at him and simply said, 'I have nothing to do with this child.' She had abandoned Costel as a baby in the hospital. She herself is poor and remote from him. She couldn't accept him, she doesn't know him and could never take on the responsibility. That was the beginning and end of his family story.

Relationship as the bread of life

After four years' work in Rumania we have built a village for the street children, we run a small social centre at the station in Bucharest, and have a couple of homes in the city in which children and young people are to experience and get something of what we have experienced and got from our families. Of course this is a drop in the ocean – we have room for around 150 children. Every day children still run up to me and my colleagues, clutch our hands and beg, 'I want to live with you, I want to go to the farm for the children.' And we have to say no and put them off with some chewing gum. These are difficult situations. Have we nothing to give the children to whom we cannot offer a home or a bed? If we can do nothing else, we go in small groups every day at a particular time to a metro station at a place in the station to bring the children an apple or a roll.

But in reality we are also bringing them something quite different and they also expect something quite different: a family, a relationship. We notice that they are angry when we're late and embrace us wildly. The relationship is the important thing. This struck me one night in the late autumn when I found children barefoot in the station and asked them jokingly, 'What shall I bring you?', expecting that they would want shoes. But they said, 'No, bring us a ball to play with.' They wanted to play, they wanted a relationship, they wanted people with whom they could be children and enjoy themselves and not be exploited. I like to mark the foreheads of the children I can't take with me with the sign of the cross, and sense how much they like having it, how secure they then feel, although they will be left behind. It then often happens that quite deliberately they make the sign of the cross on my forehead, so to speak as a gift in return.

Once a girl whispered in my ear, 'I'm praying for you.' This experience of play and the sign and the religious continues in our small houses for the children, where they argue about whether one makes the sign of the cross from left to right or from right to left, i.e. according to the Latin or the Greek rite, and where they like nothing so much as a song, especially a religious song or a prayer. They show an openness and a hunger and a readiness for faith which far exceeds anything that I have ever found in prosperous Western society. I conclude from this that despite all the material need to be met, the main task consists in meeting the cultural, spiritual, religious family need and satisfying the need for a link, giving the children an inner home (and that is a bond between East and West, between a prosperous society and a poor society), which we can provide through religion and culture, through the sign and the family and our relationship.

Here the material plays a necessary but ambivalent role. It is necessary, because otherwise relations become difficult, because a child cannot be accepted and healed if it has no house, no bed, no warmth. But it is dangerous when it replaces the spiritual. It is open to misunderstanding because it often conceals the deeper longing and makes the poor children even poorer, in that they suddenly find themselves swimming in gifts from aid that they can't cope with; here the neglect, the neglect of them as human beings, gets even worse. The material is dangerous because one has to learn to deal with it first, and we ourselves have to understand that it is only the presupposition for what the children really want of us: a relationship, security, a home, meaning in life, religion. The real task of the church must be never to lose sight of this task and this ultimate goal, and this is a task of which neither a state nor even an international organization can relieve it.

The children whom I have been describing are often called 'nobody's children' in Rumania. Positively speaking, this means that our task and the task of the church is to give each of them a father, a mother, a sister, a brother – and that is more than the material.

The 'latchkey children' in a prosperous society correspond to the 'nobody's children' of a poor society. A year ago with a group of helpers I undertook to develop a parish on the edge of Vienna. This parish came into being within two years. Homes for 15,000 were and are being built on green fields. The key figures in this parish are the children, because the population consists almost entirely of young couples with children. Many parents are foreigners, who are working in Vienna above all in the caring professions and therefore get a community house. Their children suddenly appear in church. Recently two girls were sitting in the front row and I asked them (this was at Pentecost), 'What language do you know?', because it was quite clear from their complexions that they didn't just speak German. One said, 'I also know Filipino', and the other said 'Hindu' – those were their words. I asked them before the assembled congregation, 'How did you find the church? Why are you here?' They replied, 'The doors were open and we simply walked in!' I was delighted at this and said so, and the whole congregation made the children feel how glad they were to have them. Since then the children have been coming regularly.

We now experience similar stories every day. Children come to the church doors with bicycles or skateboards because there's a nice open space there and one can do all kinds of manoeuvres on the steps. We talk to them, play with them and also ask whether they would like to take part in the service. We have ministries to offer. That causes a furore. On Sunday we have to limit the number of ministers to twelve. But many also come to minister on weekdays. And our work begins by showing them how to do it. It is their ambition to do it right, genuflecting and doing other things in worship. Since then new children have been coming every day and with them their parents, who after being accepted by the church want to be baptized.

Living in the church

The most important point is that the children, for whom the parents often have little time for economic or professional reasons, look for security, a family and even more a role. They want to minister, serve, take on a role in the world and also have a role before God, to serve God. The devotion and piety with which they do this leaves no doubt about this human longing which is so manifest in our children. The secret consists in having a role, in praise of God, in service of others and of society, through being able to live in the church which is open, which has no office hours or closing times. In this it is like a family in which the mother also has no opening hours and no closing times, even if she has to ask for consideration and has limits. It is this living in the church which is always open for all that our children look for and find.

And the grown-up children?

Before I came to deal with children, I was entrusted with the homeless, older and younger people who had landed on the streets as a result of criminality, illness, alcoholism or drug problems. I found my best and most personal friends there. They were all sick, difficult, unattractive. They seemed powerful and often also terrifying to citizens. But I have to say that they were like children. They looked for a relationship, a meaning in life, feeling, tenderness, and all the violence was merely a protective measure so that they didn't have to show this real longing. These children are the most difficult that I have encountered because at first glance they arouse no pity. They are poor and lonely, but in need of protection. The church may be their advocate; in them it can see the presence of Jesus and also give to those who have more good fortune in life. What the children in East and West, big and small, seek and long for can be summed up like this: 'What I seek is a role, is protection, security, dignity, because that is how God has made me and guided my way to the present.'

The church is the advocate of children. That is true equally of the situation in both East and West, though the challenges in poor and threatened countries are not like those in rich and secure countries. The church is aware that the so-called Akedah, the 'binding' of Isaac, is a symbol of its task. Isaac had to be bound by Abraham to indicate that the tribal ancestor has to sacrifice everything, even his beloved child, and moreover the child of the promise, his only child given him contrary to all expectations at the age of 100. Abraham has no right to him. God alone has a right to Isaac. And this God sends his messenger with the news that children may not be victims: the symbol that they belong to God is to stamp your liturgy.

At the time of Jesus the people of Israel was suspected of rebelliousness and stupidity by the pagan Roman empire because they rejected the power of adults over children which applied under Roman law. Children in the Roman empire had no rights. The family decided whether there should be an abortion, whether a child that was born should be brought up or exposed. The Jews were mocked by Roman poets and writers like Virgil and Tacitus because they brought up *all* their children (in order, it was thought, that their people would grow) instead of deciding as adults whether the children were useful and important politically, economically or within the family. The people of Israel among whom Jesus experienced and learned his relationship between adults and children had a feast of Hanukkah, a feast of lights at the winter solstice (interestingly, with a parallel in the later Christian feast of Christmas, which is also about the dignity of the child, the dignity of Jesus the new-born in the manger in Bethlehem), at which the dignity and inviolability of the child was defended.

The role of children has remained the same to the present day. They are exposed to the powerful, but they are also indicators of justice and injustice, of the quality or failure of a social system. However powerful the economy becomes, it cannot get hold of the children: that is our experience both in Rumania and in the new suburb of Vienna.

Footnote

In the years since it has been opened up, Rumania has become famous or notorious for its street children. The Rumanians suffer as a result of this, it understandably offends them, for it would not do justice to Austria to speak only of the drug addicts or to Germany to speak only of the children of the Zoo station. On the other hand there is perhaps a great opportunity for Rumania in this sorry fame, for if it succeeds in coping with this problem with the help of those of us who come from abroad and have been accepted there, I am sure that the exodus, the way to freedom, will be guaranteed. The fate of the 'nobody's children' is a reliable criterion for Rumania's way into the future. We must remember the many children in Rumania whom I have encountered who are in a better position, ready to learn and prepared to set out, even if they speak less to our feelings. Through my work with the street children and the years I was able to spend in Rumania, I have come to know children and young people of the kind I have yet to meet in the rich West. A sensitive, lively youth is ready to start off, and they will become an elite and exercise leadership if they are given a little help, perhaps from the West.

Translated by John Bowden

Learning to Live and Believe with Children

Norbert Mette

Children – objects or subjects in (religious) education?

'Do dogs have wings in heaven?' 'Jesus' surname is God.' When adults quote these and similar remarks of children which are typical of children's thought and children's ideas about religious matters,[1] there are often all kinds of overtones. They extend from amazement at the concrete and inventive way in which children develop their pictures of God and the angels, heaven and earth, to a degree of amusement about the naivety which is expressed in them. However, such remarks are not usually taken really seriously. For the widespread prejudice is that children cannot yet cope with such questions; they are merely repeating in their own way what they have picked up from adults. Adults are even more at a loss when (their) children confront them seriously with religious questions, especially if for example they are parents who want their children to grow up as far as possible in a 'religionless' way, perhaps because they themselves have bad memories of their own religious socialization or for other reasons, and now see their intentions persistently questioned by their own children. They suddenly have to react to the questions and views of the children, but do not know how. All at once they themselves have to become clearer about questions and things in a sphere which hitherto they had largely suppressed from their life.[2]

These two examples show that what F. Schweitzer has called 'the religion of the child' is clearly full of tensions. On the one hand, even now it is not taken really seriously by adults, but is dismissed as naive. The conclusion that is then drawn is that if children are to become 'properly' religious they must be brought up that way. On the other hand, children prove to be in a position to entangle themselves and adults in questions which are far from being childishly easy and which therefore cannot simply be avoided. Don't the children all at once begin to 'bring up' adults here in a religious way? As largely in education generally, in religious education, too, a view of upbringing dominated and still dominates, according to which it is the adults who have to familiarize growing children with the knowledge and capacities that they need if they are to be able to orientate themselves and act as adults in society. This view was, and to a degree still is, rooted all the more deeply in the sphere of religious education in particular, since this has been, and is, regarded as a process of handing on revealed truths to which each new generation can only be introduced and in which it has to be instructed. As previous articles in this issue have shown, both the pedagogical reflections arising from present insights into the development of children and anthropological, theological reflections on childhood suggest that such views should be fundamentally revised. Children can no longer be regarded as being to some degree defective human beings who first need to be brought up to become full personalities. From the beginning they are actively involved in the 'construction of reality'. 'More recent research shows us the child as a being with an active and creative concern to evoke meaning together with others; it is therefore concerned for mutuality and lasting communication, and wants to invest in that.'[3] Upbringing is accordingly to be defined as a social, interactive process in which both adults and children are involved and which the construction of a 'meaningful world of shared significances' (U. Peukert) takes place.

Ursula Peukert has shown the degree to which those who bring up children are involved in this effort to open up the space that children need to develop their capacities by indicating the tension which they experience as adults: 'On the one hand it is important to recognize the child's own activities and thus see it as a person in its own right from the beginning (H. Stierlin). On the other hand the adult must also constantly act as a representative of the child and anticipate its future development; the adult is then in danger of either manipulating the child according to his or her own unfulfilled wishes and projections or exposing it directly to the pressure of social expectations.'[4] Everyone who has tried to become involved with children in this way knows that they themselves emerge from this encounter different from what they were when they began, and that their own identity therefore undergoes a sustained development. So there is more truth in the saying that children 'bring up' adults than is generally supposed. And this is also – and not least – true in respect of religion.

This much can already be inferred from these reflections: any process of upbringing which seeks to set growing children free for their freedom and not determine them in a given direction has a religious dimension in the widest sense, to the degree that inevitably questions about the meaning of life and the world are raised.[5] So this is also the sphere where religious education already has to begin, namely by helping to allow such questions without the immediate need to go on to find answers to them; indeed, such education must make possible experiences in dealings with one another and in the construction of reality which allows questions of meaning and significance to arise.

I shall now attempt to sketch out the main goals and tasks which arise for religious education in respect of both adults and children. For reasons of space, by way of an example I must concentrate on the infant stage, or elementary education.[6]

The challenge to adults

Problems with religious education have to do not so much with children – on the contrary, they are very receptive in this respect – as with adults. For as is well known, religion or faith cannot be taught like writing or calculating. Anyone who wants to communicate something to children here gets personally entangled in the subject-matter and personally confronts the question of his or her attitude to religion. The children sense very quickly when adults are putting something to them which does not represent their standpoint. If, for example, when they ask where God is, they are put off with the banal answer that God is everywhere, they notice that for adults this question is obviously not a question, or that adults suppress it with all their might.

To put things another way, this means that first adults must be put in a position of being able to argue with themselves and sort out their own ideas and attitudes. Here work with parents and further training of teachers is helpful. This needs to be done in such a way that they are not instructed 'from outside', but can openly exchange their questions and doubts, anxieties and hopes etc. The topic is not what religion or faith is, but how these have been and are being experienced in their own biography. Only when, for example, open talk is possible about how much in retrospect the religion conveyed in childhood and youth has been felt to be so constricting and alienating that it needs to be left behind if life is to be lived truly, can a new way to religion or faith perhaps be found, and different experiences in this sphere be perceived.

These could then be sparked off, for example, in the following way. Bringing children into the world and nurturing them raises the question what this is good for. The answer must – as M. J. Langeveld once remarked – be put in terms of ultimate risk. But how is that possible – especially at a time when the future is felt to be as uncertain and full of risks as it is today? However, not only the future is in question. Here adults must also ask themselves what is so important and valuable to them that they want to hand it on to the next generation for their lives.

Of course many more superficial problems arise in everyday upbringing, and these must be solved just as much as the deeper questions. Nevertheless, whether such questions are dealt with and how, whether they are allowed or constantly suppressed, whether they are struggled with or regarded as unimportant, has an effect on this normal everyday life. To some degree the adult's own 'dogmas of life' are being discussed here. What am I bringing my child up for and how am I dealing with it? What does it mean to want the best for one's child? Does it mean to spoil it or to deny it things? And how do adults deal with consumerism and asceticism?

If one then becomes clear that the question of the unconditional ultimately relates to a religious level, it can perhaps also become clear that religious education is not the separate sector in dealing with children that it is often thought to be, but touches on the basic questions of upbringing – understood as making possible shared life in the future. And as a decision has always already been taken on these basic questions in practical everyday education, it is all the more important for it to be discussed explicitly every now and then. It then has to be shown whether, and to what degree, helpful suggestions and perspectives can be offered by the religious traditions, perhaps in the way in which they put in question some things that are taken for granted or oppose them, and thus represent a challenge. That here we are dealing with children, in a situation where such questions can be particularly oppressive, makes the confidence of the gospel that they can proclaim the kingdom of God to us adults quite concrete.

Stages of development in life – and faith

Often enough in nurture, religion has become the scapegoat for curtailing the elementary needs of children and limiting their emotions and motivations in order to bring them into line with the behaviour and thought desired by adults. It is no coincidence that people with a religious upbringing are often unable to show spontaneous feelings: at a very early age they are trained in moderation and balance in this area. By contrast, children have almost a 'natural' understanding of God as the giver and creator who has entrusted human beings with the continuation of his work. However, those who have never been allowed to try out their creative powers can hardly find an existential approach to this statement of faith. This example is representative of the various realms of experience in which the child lives, and which it encounters in a religious experience, above all in the first years of life: giving children room which takes account of their needs for development, in which they can develop their spiritual and emotional capacities, in which they can follow the pressure to discover their environment and turn to others is important. Outside this sphere of course there must be people with whom children 'can discuss their experiences, to whom they dare to entrust their anxieties and cares, and who recognize their individual progress in knowledge and feeling'.[7] Only in such dealing with children which allows their curiosity to come into play, which gives them confidence to turn to adults with their question of where things come from and where they are going, in the feeling that their concerns will be understood, can a sense of what religion can mean for a child at this early age be developed.

This begins with apparently small details, but these are great steps forward for children and adults do not always make things easy for them. One decisive step in their development of self is learning to say 'no' as a presupposition of being able to say 'yes'. If it is allowed, this 'no' can liberate creative forces because it makes distinctions necessary: things are not just accepted as they are, but are reacted against and possibly resisted. A further step in the genesis of an autonomous I-authority is the capacity to be able to say 'I', an I which has a will of its own and is different from others. These stages of development go in anything but a straight line; here the child is torn to and fro by ambivalent feelings and conflicts: it fluctuates between fantasies of omnipotence and experiences of impotence, between helplessness and a demonstration of independence, between identification with those to whom it relates and aggressions, between love and hate. It feels anxiety in every degree of intensity – anxiety about survival and about losses. Becoming independent and nevertheless being able to have good, trustworthy relations with others proves to be a highly contradictory task, yet one which is vitally necessary.

In all this the ideas of small children in particular, their thought, is largely bound up with practical achievement: it is a 'logic of doing'. And yet this logic does not end up in doing. The action of children is in no way merely instrumental; it is essentially communicative action. In other words, it is concerned to come to terms with its environment, not to conquer it. This finds paradigmatic expression in play. That explains why the significance of action for the child is not exhausted in the action itself – for example when it has achieved a purpose – but goes deeper. 'Every concept, every sentence, but also non-verbal elements of expression, facial expressions and gestures, indeed even whole conversational situations that the child experiences, as at the family table, when cleaning teeth, when the father [or the mother] says good-bye, parting from father and mother at the kindergarten door, saying good night, take on a content additional to the objective one accessible to anyone, which gives them a special character. It comprises both additional cognitive meanings and also emotional moods, inclinations and antipathies, and attaches these forms of expression and communicative scenes to particular relations between persons.'[8] In this way elementary symbols come into being which accompany the whole of further development; they can support, but also hinder, if they have robbed bad experiences of their outcome.

Tasks for an explicit religious upbringing at an infant stage

What tasks are involved in an explicit religious upbringing at this age? I preface the following remarks with a question from Hartmut von Hentig which takes up what has just been said and develops it in connection with our question: 'Children are innocent. They are convinced that they can do what they want. They paint a battleship, grandmother in the wolf's mouth, God in the burning bush. They do not have the despair, the timidity, the mistrust which go with an adult experiential wisdom. They do not just believe; their life is wholly faith.'[9]

1. *The elementary experience of unconditionally being accepted and wanted*

It is remarkable how much in the religions, and particularly also in Christianity, traditional knowledge takes up the basic experiences and conflicts of early childhood and preserves and expresses them in many of its symbols. To this degree believing is already touched on by these experiences and conflicts. This is especially true of the fundamental experience of being unconditionally accepted and wanted, which is fundamental to the further crisis of development. Where these experiences of being absolutely affirmed and loved are handed on in practice, faith already comes about in an elementary way; after all, this experience lies at its heart. On this basis an interpretation of this practice which does justice to the child's development, an explanation of faith in God as the support of all being, can then be offered and communicated, and by means of the symbols and narratives that are handed on, the promising experiences of interaction in early childhood can be transformed into eschatological hopes beyond childhood. Here is a place for the telling of stories from the Bible, if the stories enable children also to discover themselves in them. Praying also becomes an important ritual into which children can be drawn if it includes the experiences of the day, so that life can be expressed in an elementary way before God with its anxieties, joys and conflicts – in praise and petition, thanksgiving and lament.

2. Developing a sense of the many dimensions of reality

It is typical of small children that they can immerse themselves completely in what they are doing, e.g. playing or looking at something. For their development, and also for their religious development, much depends on whether they are allowed time and corresponding stimuli to enable them to learn to see with what H. Halbfas has called the 'third eye'. In this way they learn not only to take the given as the real but also to get a sense of its many dimensions and also give dreams and longings their due. The stimulation of fantasies and the encouragement of their own creativity are also fundamental dimensions of religious upbringing, and these do not begin with the mere reception and consumption of what is offered from elsewhere but from the possibility of making something – something new out of what is there.

3. Learning justice

A pernicious reduction of religious education which can frequently be encountered is that from an early age it is kept to 'prayer' and leaves out or puts in the background 'doing right'. Both belong together, as Dietrich Bonhoeffer described in an impressive way in the letter to his godson Dietrich Bethge.[10] Here he emphasized that learning to do right and, as a presupposition for this, first opening one's eyes to others must be perceived and taken seriously as an essential task of religious education, which follows from love of God and the neighbour. Here, too, practical dealings with children – namely whether they are recognized as being different and other, are taken seriously and thus enabled to recognize others – can become a test case. Children possibly show themselves the best teachers when it is a matter of being fair to others. For example, children do not understand why their contemporaries have to live in poverty and wretchedness, why they are robbed of their childhood, indeed why all over the world 40,000 children die every day. They look questioningly at adults, asking what kind of a world we have made for them, and in their spontaneous readiness to share demonstrate that things could be different and fairer in this world.[11]

Safeguarding elementary experiences of childhood[12]

Doesn't what has been said here about religious upbringing presuppose something like a 'whole world' (of children) of a kind that does not exist (any longer)? Isn't it an illusion from the start? If we think, for example, of the symbols which the Christian message has accepted in order to explain what the issues are or were for men and women (of the time) and bring them near to experience – light and darkness, water and wind, bread and wine, etc. – mustn't the possibility of being able to experience them at all be brought about artificially today? Where does life with brothers and sisters or a continuing relationship to a father or mother form part of the experience of today's children? Doesn't that mean that religious education which presupposes this inevitably becomes a possible special realm within dealings with children which otherwise are not influenced by it?

In return, however, we must ask where upbringing then leads to. Doesn't it all too easily deteriorate into being conditioned by the existing situation, a one-dimensional reduction of human beings in which the important thing is to nip the fantasies and longings of childhood in the bud? If we do not want simply to bow to the *Diktat* of prevailing circumstances, then religious education takes on an explosive character of its own: it can neither exhaust itself in the mere transmission of traditional religious forms of life (in the social reserves which are set apart for this), nor can it merely – as so often in history – contribute to the reproduction of the members necessary for present social conditions. It is a necessary interruption and transformation of what has previously been taken for granted, in the direction of a society in which the possibilities of people's experience in dealing with themselves, one another, nature and in all this with God, are not unnecessarily constricted and alienated any longer. Such a definition of tasks may sound unusual to current religious educationalists. Yet this is quite simply the obvious consequence of the statement that with the undermining of presuppositions for religious education goes a danger to the development of children's spheres of perception and capacities for experience. So religious education means making a contribution towards cleaning up the worlds in which children live – and thus society generally.[13]

If children were to make the church . . . [14]

According to Paulo Freire, processes of upbringing and learning which do not keep children under the thumb but seek to further their development towards the autonomy which first makes them capable of really recognizing others are bound up with a particular form of life which he calls 'convivence' or 'conviviality'. This originally denotes a way of living together which can be found above all in the cultures of simple people characterized by a practice of sharing in solidarity, from helping one another, through learning from one another, to celebrating with one another.[15] Within the framework of Freire's pedagogy, convivence denotes 'the learning community of those who want to learn from each other and with each other for a human life. In a community of convivence learnt knowledge does not have priority over experiential knowledge. In the process of learning together, latent knowledge is exposed and new knowledge produced. Creative possibilities and social sensibility are discovered and introduced into a common plan. Teachers and learners together share in this convivence.'[16] In short, this is the practice of learning which overlaps generations.

Such places or spheres of convivence are characteristic forms of life for traditional societies, and their existence can no longer be presupposed in modern society. On the contrary, they have been largely overrun by the process of 'the colonialization of life-worlds' (Habermas). Yet the question arises with increasing urgency whether modern society is not also dependent for its future on such 'sociotopes' and the learning in inter-subjective creativity practised in them.[17]

In this context it might seem natural to point to local churches as possible places for such convivence. Good reasons can be adduced for this in view of their role and also their beginnings. Nevertheless, an effusive optimism which thinks it can outdo the concrete constitution of these churches is hardly in place. We must note soberly that the Catholic Church in particular, with its concern to communicate faith in a motivated way to the rising generation, to a considerable degree itself stands in the way. Certainly there are factors of social change which can hardly be influenced directly by the church, like the trend towards an individualized religion and the consequence that individuals themselves increasingly determine how they will be committed to the church. Nevertheless, the church has apparently failed to understand how to accept these changes productively, but instead has stubbornly insisted on a compulsive defence of its status. The consequence is, among other things, an abysmal alienation of the world in which people live from the world of faith, which makes young parents, for example, helpless over the religious interests of their children.[18]

Possibly here, too, children could also start a healthy process of conversion in local churches and communities. In a report of efforts at community practice along these lines in Amsterdam, Jan Nieuwenhuis has shown that an option for a church community with children in no way makes the community 'childish' but confronts it with basic questions about its existence and mission: 'A community with children, and pastoral work for children, is not an optional matter. It is not a question of new skills or new techniques. Anyone who decides for the children chooses a new world. Chooses the poor and the smallest and those without rights and the handicapped. He or she chooses another society and a new church. One cannot take children seriously in worship and at the same time want – for example – foreign workers to be deported without further ado. Anyone who does this does not know what a child is. Therefore pastoral work for children is a tricky matter and like a knife in the soul . . . Those who embark on a liturgy with children should know that they will burn their wings and in so doing "change their lives" (Mark 1.15). They will experience that this transforms the face of the church community, that structures become questionable and that really before one knows it a revolution has begun with oneself and one's church . . . Anyone who wants to have a message for children in the church discovers that this message overturns everything: language, customs, rites, ourselves. Much changes when one begins on that. Everything really. A new world dawns.'[19]

Translated by John Bowden

Notes

1. Collections of such sayings are popular, e.g. H. and J. Zink, *Kriegt ein Hund in Himmel Flügel?*, Freiburg 1972; M. A. Albane, *Jesus hiess mit Nachnamen Gott*, Frankfurt am Main 1994.
2. Cf. M. Fay, *Brauchen Kinder Religion?*, Hamburg 1994.
3. U. Peukert, 'Erziehung in der frühen Kindheit', in D. Englehard et al. (eds.), *Handbuch der Elementarerziehung*, Seelze 1994, no page numbers.
4. Ibid.
5. See here N. Mette, *Religionspädagogik*, Düsseldorf 1994, esp. 102ff.
6. For what follows, in addition to the literature mentioned in the notes see

R. Coles, *Wird Gott nass, wenn es regnet?* *Die religiöse Bilderwelt der Kinder*, Hamburg 1992; *Der evangelische Erzieher* 44, 1992, 3, *Kind und Religion;* Der evangelische Erzieher 45, 1993, 4, *Frauen: Religion und Sozialisation*; V. Merz (ed.), *Alter Gott für neue Kinder?*, Fribourg 1994; K. E. Nipkow, 'Anfänge gemeinsamen Lebens und Glaubens – zum Beitrag des Kindergartens', in id., *Bildung als Lebensbegleitung und Erneuerung*, Gütersloh 1990, 301–22: 365; *Religionspädagogische Beiträge* 35, 1995: *Kindsein heute*; F. Schweitzer, *Die Religion des Kindes*, Gütersloh 1992; Synode der Evangelischen Kirche in Deutschland, *Aufwachsen in schwieriger Zeit – Kinder in Gemeinde und Gesellschaft*, Gütersloh 1995.

7. L. Krappmann, 'Bedürfnisse der Kinder respektieren', *Welt des Kindes* 57, 1970, 46.

8. L. Krappmann, 'Symbole, Riten, Festlichkeit', in Caritas-Verband fur die Diözese Münster (ed.), *Religiöse Erziehung und christliche Gemeinde*, Münster 1981, 15–33: 23.

9. H. von Gentig, 'Der glimmende Docht, Oder: Seht, die Kinder!' *NS* 27, 1987, 459–80: 479.

10. Cf. D. Bonhoeffer, *Letters and Papers from Prison, The Enlarged Edition*, London and New York 1971, 294ff., esp. 298.

11. For more detail see N. Mette, 'Gerechtigkeit lernen – die religionspädagogische Aufgabe', *RPB* 27, 1991, 3–26; id., 'Subjektwerden an den und mit den anderen', *EE* 43, 1991, 620–30.

12. For what follows see in more detail N. Mette, *Voraussetzungen christlicher Elementarerziehung*, Düsseldorf 1983, esp. 330–5 and the important texts and standpoints in *Aufwachsen in schwieriger Zeit* (n. 6).

13. Cf. L. Krappmann, 'Über die Zukunft der Kindheit: Herausforderungen und Perspektiven in einen vereinten Deutschland', in S. Ebert (ed.), *Zukunft für Kinder*, Münich 1991, 253–66; cf. also the statement by G. Becker, H. von Hentig and J. Zimmer, 'Die Verantwortung der Christen für die Kinder und ihre Zukunft', *NS* 27, 1987, 495–500.

14. Cf. in more detail N. Mette, 'Kinder', in C. Bäumler and id. (ed.), *Gemeindepraxis in Grundbegriffen*, Munich and Düsseldorf 1987, 228–38.

15. The origin and background to this concept is explained by T. Sudermeier, 'Konvivenz als Grundstruktur ökumenischer Existenz heute', in W. Huber et al., *Ökumenische Existenz heute* 1, Munich 1986, 49–100, esp. 52ff.

16. W. Huber, 'Bedrohte Welt und christliche Glabe – Herausforderung für Lehrende und Lernende', in R. Becker et al. (ed.), *Mensch und Christ in der Schule*, Paderborn 1988, 61–82: 82.

17. Cf. U. Becker, 'Heutige Schüler und Schülerinnen und die alte Religion?', in *anr-Rundschreiben* no. 23, January 1991, 25–36, esp. 31ff.

18. Cf. A. Dubach, 'Wie denken junge Eltern über Religion und Kirche?', in W. Simon and M. Delgado (eds.), *Lernorte des Glaubens*, Berlin-Hildesheim 1991, 69–96.

19. J. Nieuwenhuis, 'Das Kind wird Euch weiden. Perspektiven einer kinderfreundlichen Pastoral', in J. H. Wiener and H. Erharter (eds.), *Kinderpastoral*, Vienna 1982, 75–93: 85; cf. also the basic text (working paper) of the National Conference of Brazilian Bishops on the 1987 Campaign for Brotherhood, *Whoever*

Receives a Little Child Receives Me. The title of this article is formulated on the terms 'learning to live and believe together' coined by K. E. Nipkow, *Grundfragen der Religionspädagogik*, Vol. 3, Gütersloh 1982, 30.

Children in the Liturgy – Initiation and Participation

Birgit Jeggle-Merz

Parents are often faced with a lack of enthusiasm when they say to their children, 'Now we're going to church.' Children usually find worship boring, tough going, and meaningless. As a rule they don't feel that they are part of the celebration, that they are really involved; at best they feel onlookers. But the celebration of the death and resurrection of Jesus Christ in its manifold dimensions is not an incidental which Christianity could dispense with or delegate to those who are specially called to it. On the contrary, the celebration of faith in the saving message of Jesus Christ is the foundation of our religious life, the basis of the life of the church community and as it were its climax. In going on to speak of the 'initiation', in other words of the 'introduction', of children into the celebration of liturgy, my concern will not be with the continuation of a two-thousand-year-old tradition which seems necessary for reasons of piety to the past; rather, I am quite certain that liturgy is life and seeks to communicate life. If that is the case, then the participation of children in this life-giving liturgy is not an incidental matter, a kind of occupational therapy that can be dropped or replaced, but a constitutive part of the nature of liturgy and Christianity.

The connection between liturgy and life

There is a widespread view, not only among younger church members but also in the wider (and sometimes even in the narrower) circles of the church, that the church's liturgy is a dull, outdated ritual. Given this view, the relationship between liturgy and life is by no means evident at first sight. The complaint is that because the social framework of liturgy has changed in a way which is described with phrases like 'the anonymity of the everyday world', 'privatization', 'the influence of the media and the consumer society', 'excessive demands on small families', and so on, the liturgy can no longer give the answer to human questions. Moreover, after the comprehensive reform following Vatican II, the liturgy is said to have been 'disenchanted', 'demythologized', 'made too wordy' – in other words, robbed of its power. Today our daily life is not in fact governed by faith in God's guidance and in the death and resurrection of Jesus Christ (far less by the celebration of this faith). Moreover membership of a church community is no longer a social requirement, as it still was twenty years ago. So on closer inspection it becomes clear that belief has become the most private concern of the individual. What role does the liturgy of the church still play in it? Must it merely represent the place in which individuals are given the ritual background for their discovery of themselves and in which account is therefore taken of their need of the mythical, the religious, the occult and the esoteric?[1] If we were to answer this question in the affirmative, in my view we would not need to reflect further on introducing our children to the liturgy as the communal celebration of the assembled community.

Over against this stands the knowledge and the experience that human beings need a visible, tangible church which they can experience in order to be able to believe and give this faith concrete expression in their lives. A twofold dimension in the religious socialization[2] of men and women is indispensable, and this can be found only in the liturgy: men and women want to be seen as individuals, as persons, and to find their own personal answers to God's call, while at the same time they have a need to belong to a community of like-minded people. The church's liturgy symbolizes such a community, which offers security and stability through its inner structure (which is also hierarchical) and its two thousand-year-old history. In this church men and women are both individuals before their God and at the same time individuals among many. It is clear from the split between worship and everyday life which is bewailed in many places that human beings long to be able to experience both dimensions: in other words, the church has something personal to do with me; it gives me an answer to the questions of my life. At the same time the church weaves me into a community which takes me beyond the subjectivity of my individual being and gives me extra meaning as part of this community. Where this happens, where the church clearly becomes this, is primarily where it prays. One can experience in liturgical celebration that God is a God who acts in human beings because here God turns to them and involves them in

God's history (of salvation). In this way the human being becomes the real and true contemporary of God's action (in salvation) and does not remain someone born too late, who can only commemorate events which happened two thousand years ago and more. Nowhere else than in the liturgy does it become evident that God's saving acts are not things of the past, and have by no means lost their power even today. In the liturgy we have to experience the possibility of what it means to be disciples of this Jesus Christ (in every sense of the word), through whose death and resurrection we can only achieve what being a Christian and not least being human means: salvation and eternal life. In the celebration of the mystery of the resurrection of Jesus Christ it becomes clear that we do not lag behind those who could experience the acts of God themselves but are truly contemporaries of God's action.[3]

So the church is not just any institution, but an eminent place at which men and women can encounter God. Even today, as always, the celebration of the liturgy is the heart of the church; in other words, anyone who wants to experience the church and live by its sources needs the celebration of the liturgy. Being a Christian without being linked to the celebration of the death and resurrection as a central celebration of the mysteries has no foundation and support, since the liturgy is never something in itself, but the place where men and women stand before their God, who wishes things to be well with them and shows them the way to salvation. In this sense liturgy is life: not a worn-out ritual that has to be performed, but real life with Christ and the church that it can communicate and give to those who celebrate it. It is a life behind which stand both God and humankind, a life in which they can encounter each other. This life cannot be explained in a few words, but it can be experienced in the liturgy, because here it has been given a name: commemoration of the saving acts of God and the human response to these acts.[4]

The significance of worship for the life of the church – liturgy as a reflection of the life of the community

The tension between commitment and freedom, the interaction of a community with the forms that have grown up and contain a great treasure of experience, and the quest for authentic answers to the questions of the time, is something which runs right through the history of Christian worship. So concern for a way of worshipping which corresponds to what we are today is not a new thing in our time. The liturgy has paramount importance in forming the community and the church and at the same time shaping and supporting it, and without it the church and thus the faithful cannot live. No other expression of the life of the church is so much an expression of church identity as the liturgy, so much so that today we speak of 'eucharistic ecclesiology'.[5] That means that the church (both world church and local church) builds itself on the Sunday celebration of the eucharist and manifests itself in it (cf. SC 7, LG 11).[6]

The Second Vatican Council has clearly and unmistakably indicated that the whole community is the bearer and subject of the liturgy on the basis of the common priesthood of all who have been baptized and confirmed. The participation of the faithful in the liturgy is not something additional for them, but is already a necessary part of their existence. The church is formed by the individual celebrating communities assembled for worship, people who can live as Christians in the world on the basis of this action, and in the union of the different celebrating communities in the one eucharist all over the world. It is the liturgy, not the ministries and their organization, which lies at the heart of the church. According to the present-day understanding determined by the Second Vatican Council, worship is more than the officially regulated cult; it is a reflection of the whole of church life, indeed at the same time the source and climax of community life (SC 10). Accordingly, an act of worship can never stand on its own, can never be an isolated event, but needs to be related to a community and must reflect the actual conditions in the church, its faith and its life. So liturgical renewal is a constant process which is only possible when there is constant attention and readiness to engage in it.

A liturgy which does justice to children does justice to all

What have these basic reflections on the nature of the liturgy and its significance for church and community to do with our topic of the initiation and participation of children in the liturgy? Their purpose was to clarify what is indispensable to the building up and the life of a community – to which children also belong. The community assembles, sure in its faith, confesses and celebrates this faith, and in this way is strengthened and enabled for the tasks which arise from this faith. An isolated consideration of 'the child and worship' does not go far enough, unless it has first clarified where the child is to be led, why it is important for children to have positive experiences in the celebration of worship. There is no dispute that now and then special worship can be held for and with particular groups in the community, for the old, the young, women, the handicapped and also for children. The problem is that no special account is taken of these 'groups' – including children – in the other 'normal' (i.e. regular) forms of worship.

Given this suggestion, what direction should further reflections take? On the one hand it is important to make it possible for children to have experience in worship which can shape their whole understanding of the church and faith. Those who reflect on their own 'liturgical biographies' will easily see that there were important key experiences in their lives that were directly connected with liturgical celebration and made a decisive contribution to their still remaining members of the church. So any effort to enable our children to have such experiences can only be welcomed. On the other hand, this reflection does not go far enough, for just as life does not consist only of high points, so the situation in our churches every day and every week is not to be underestimated: it is often indicated there to children that there is no place for their needs and wishes. However, on closer inspection it emerges that sufficient attention is not always paid to the needs and wishes of the old, youth, women and handicapped (and probably also men) either; otherwise the impression could not arise that worship is boring and passes over real life. So it is all too understandable that children clearly indicate that they want to be taken as subjects of liturgy and members of the community in their own right (by saying 'I don't like church. I get nothing out of it'). However, if liturgical life is embedded in the life of the whole community, if the Sunday eucharist is in fact an assembly of the whole community and a high point of its life, the danger of going over the heads of those involved will be less.

Thus on closer inspection the desire for a liturgy which does justice to children corresponds to the desire for the needs and questions of all to be heard and for all to be able to bring these needs and questions before God.

Involving children in worship

If so far I have given the impression that one need not pay special attention to children in the liturgical life of a community, then I will have been misunderstood. It is right and necessary to heed the needs, requirements and possibilities of children, to take note of them and integrate them into the shaping of worship. Not only so that children can enjoy taking part in worship more and really join in the celebration, but in order to help them to experience what believing means. In line with the title of a book by Alfred Biesinger on religious education, 'Not Deceiving Children about God',[7] I would like to talk about 'not deceiving children about ritual'. And just as

Biesinger understands his outcry as a support for parents by indicating that we can 'deprive our children of the most important experiences, namely of being loved by God and embraced by him, of having a task in this world and of bringing light to one another',[8] so I too understand 'ritual' as something which keeps recurring, which is known and brings positive experiences, something which can provide support now in difficult situations and later also in adult life.[9]

If we are talking about liturgy which does justice to children, we are not just talking about children's masses, family masses and so on. The variety of liturgical celebrations contains a treasure which is often hidden and which cannot be discovered if one simply keeps to the high form of the 'eucharist', which smaller children at least cannot grasp at all. A whole series of celebrations can be made up of less central elements – hearing the word of God, the human answer to this word and a prayer which sums up this answer.

Accordingly, the term 'children's worship' must not be limited to worship prepared specially for (only for) children (including 'toddlers' services', 'family masses', school worship and so on) but can be extended to services in which as a rule just a few children want to take part, e.g. in celebrations of baptism, in weddings, in family celebrations (for example the seventieth birthday of a grandparent), and so on. In other words, whenever there are also children in an assembly gathered for worship, these cannot simply be ignored, but must be given the opportunity really to join in celebration, to be subjects in worship in accordance with the modern understanding of worship.

It is important to observe some rules here:
– The most important criterion is authenticity. Children with their fine sensors immediately notice whether the people doing something in worship and the content of what is being conveyed to them are in tune and credible. We need not always stage something special to enthuse the children, but it is important for those involved to say and do something which rings true. This calls for real grappling with what is being thought and celebrated. It is extremely important, and not just for children, to ask what God wants to say with his word. What does this message of God mean for my personal, daily life?

Academic research into the development of faith in children points to the fundamental significance of interpersonal relations for the development of a viable form of faith. In an encounter which is stamped with authenticity and loving acceptance, it becomes possible for the child to accept what is said, done and celebrated and to rely on it. The responsibility that arises from this for us adults is not to be underestimated.

– These considerations open up our horizons to bringing the special world of children into worship. When their everyday activities, their wishes, joys and anxieties become topics, children feel that they are being taken seriously. They experience that they can bring everything that concerns them in full trust before this God and thus find confidence and help. Because we adults cannot always know what is going on inside our children, it is ideal if children can already be involved in the preparation of worship. This might seem unusual at first sight, since usually a few senior people are involved in preparing for liturgical celebrations. But one need hardly point out that ultimately this is a dead end on the way to a shared communal celebration by all members of the church.

– It is a great mistake to think that children in worship are synonymous with restlessness and/or constant action. Certainly it is less a matter of contemplation and worship than of quietness and rest. Despite (or also because of) a contrary practice which children for example encounter every day on the television, in which the attention of the viewer has to be held by constant action in sequences which get shorter and shorter, it is very important to give children the possibility of being able to 'feel their souls'. In moments of silence the important thing is not to assimilate the content of the celebration but reflect on oneself before God; this is a dimension which is not easy for us adults in view of our loud and busy world, and a situation in which we can learn a great deal from children.

– In all the literature the reader keeps encountering the demand to give total expression to faith in celebrations – but this basic insight into the need to involve body and soul is rarely put into practice. It is really quite simple: children want to touch with their hands, see with their eyes, hear with their ears, smell with their noses, taste with their palates and rejoice, dance and be themselves with their whole bodies.

It is absolutely vital for children to feel at home in worship. So here the principle 'less is more' also applies: there is no need to add to the text from Holy Scripture another story, a meditation text, or even a pious word, however profound these may be in themselves. The same goes for hymns: however popular and well sung they are, too many texts and melodies cancel each other out.

What has been said so far makes it clear that a mass in the form in which we celebrate it today can sometimes be too much for children.

– Feeling at home in worship also includes the repetition of certain prayers and formulae in worship. If children learn to pray the Our Father,

if they know what follows the invitation 'Let us pray' and so on, they learn
not only how faith can be lived but also experience it as members of a
community which is familiar to them. Furthermore, in this way they can
be introduced to the celebration of the whole community and participate in
it in a different way.

These are just a few principles for a liturgy which does justice to children;
more could be developed.[10] I would like to make one last comment:
parents keep finding their way to faith, community and church through
their children. Shaping worship in a way that does justice to children is not
just work for the youngest members of our churches, but also for their
parents.

Translated by John Bowden

Notes

1. Arno Schilson discusses this in depth. Cf. e.g. 'Liturgie und Menschsein.
Überlegungen zur Liturgiefähigkeit des Menschen am Ende des 20. Jahrhunderts',
Liturgisches Jahrbuch 39, 1989, 207–27; 'Christlicher Gottesdienst – Ort des
Menschseins. Fundamentalliturgische Überlegungen in ökumenischer Absicht', in
Gemeinsame Liturgie in getrennten Kirchen?, ed. K. Schlemmer, Freiburg, etc. 1991,
53–81.
2. Cf. e.g. the works of James W. Fowler, *Faith Development and Pastoral Care*,
Philadelphia 1987, and Fritz Oser, *Die Enstehung Gottes im Kinde: Zum Aufbau der
Gottesbeziehung in den ersten Schuljahren*, Zurich 1992.
3. This is brought out especially by Angelus A. Häussling, who links his reflections
to concrete examples from the liturgy of the church. Cf. *Liturgie: Gedächtnis eines
Vergangenen und doch Befreiung in der Gegenwart: Vom Sinn der Liturgie. Gedächtnis
unserer Erlösung und Lobpreis Gottes*, ed. A. A. Häusling, Schriften der katholischen
Akademie Bayerns 140, Düsseldorf 1991, 118–30.
4. Cf. id., 'Liturgie und Leben', *Lebendige Seelsorge* 39, 1989, 169–74.
5. Cf. Anton Thaler, *Gemeinde und Eucharistie. Grundlegung einer eucharist-
ischen Ekklesiologie*, Praktische Theologie im Dialog 2, Fribourg 1988.
6. Cf. Klemens Richter, 'Liturgiereform als Mitte einer Erneuerung der Kirche', in
*Das Konzil war erst der Anfang. Die Bedeutung des II. Vatikanums für Theologie und
Kirche*, ed. K. Richter, Mainz 1991, 53–74.
7. Albert Biesinger, *Kinder nicht um Gott betrügen. Anstiftungen für Mütter und
Väter*, Freiburg, etc. 1994.
8. Ibid., 11.
9. Heinz Vogel, 'Das eine alte tun und das andere neue lassen – das eine alte lassen
und das andere neue tun! Ein Plädoyer zu neuen Liedern einer alten Sehnsucht', *Bibel
und Liturgie* 68, 1995, 104–8.

10. Further cf. Birgit Jeggle-Merz, Ralph Sauer and Andreas Schwenzer (eds.), *Gottesdienst feiern mit Kindern. Werkbuch*, Freiburg, etc. 1994; B. Jeggle-Merz, 'Leitfaden für die Gestaltung von Kindergottesdiensten', *Bibel und Liturgie* 66, 1993, 159–64; ead., 'Das Wort Gottes im Kindergottesdienst', *Bibel und Liturgie* 68, 1995 (in preparation).

The Rights of the Child

Michael Smith Foster

Introduction

Child advocates are stereotypically divided into two mutually exclusive groups: those who promote nurturance rights and those who promote self-determination rights. Advocacy of nurturance rights involves the provision and protection of the goods and services necessary for a child's self-actualization, while advocacy of self-determination rights is based on a belief that the civil liberties accorded to adults should also be extended and proclaimed on behalf of children. Of course, when the two approaches are dichotomized into mutually exclusive camps, the advocacy is deficient. Proper advocacy is neither one nor the other, but a combination of both.

Child advocacy within legal systems should incorporate both nurturance rights and self-determination rights. In effect, children should be accorded the natural rights they possess as human persons (nurturance rights). The *exercise* of those rights should be determinative within the parameters of the family unless the law makes exceptions. Exception regarding the exercise of certain rights admits to the fact that as children mature they are able to assert their independence in some instances (self-determination rights).

With most of the nations of the world, the church has responded to the concerns of children by ratifying the United Nations Convention on the Rights of the Child. The Convention is an international human rights instrument which sets out states' obligations towards children. It is a legally binding instrument. The governments which ratify it are obliged to amend their national legislation to accommodate the provisions of the Convention and commit themselves to regular reporting on the gradual implementation of the Convention in their country.

The purpose of this presentation is to demonstrate, in a comprehensive though not exhaustive manner, the compatibility between the United Nations Convention on the Rights of Child and the law of the Roman Catholic Church.[1] The rights of children are promoted in both legal texts. This promotion is accomplished through three avenues: provision, protection and proclamation. In other words, children have the right to be provided with those things which fulfil their special needs and interests. They also have the right to be protected from harmful situations. Finally, the law proclaims they have the right to participate in decisions that affect both their individual lives and their standing in society and the church as a whole. Both legal texts also situate these rights in relation to the primacy of parental rights and the fulfilment of parental responsibilities. In essence the Convention and canon law combine nurturance and self-determination rights in a balanced perspective which supports the development of healthy families.

The following presentation will be divided into two sections. The first will address the compatibility of the articles of the Convention and the canons of the Code regarding the provision, protection and proclamation of children's rights. The second will demonstrate the compatibility of the Convention and canon law for situating children's rights within the context of the family. At the outset, it should be noted that canon law, like the Convention, defines a minor, or child, as one below the age of eighteen years (c. 97.1). Furthermore, within canon law a child below the age of seven is considered to be an infant (c. 97.2) and not bound to ecclesiastical laws (c. 11).

Convention articles and the canons of the code

First avenue of promoting children's rights: provision

Given the special needs associated with human development, children have the right to be *provided* with those goods and services necessary for their healthy maturation. Concern should be manifested not only for enhancing a child's potential as an adult, but also for recognizing a child's current experience of the world and supporting growth within the world of childhood. Hence, children should be accorded not only those rights inherent in their personhood, but other rights which accrue from their developmental needs.

The UN Convention affords children these rights. First and foremost is the right to life, survival and development (article 6). The intellectual, physical, moral, spiritual and emotional aspects of a child's life are to be nurtured (articles 23, 24, 26–32). Furthermore, children have a right to a name and nationality and to know and be cared for by their parents (article 7). Children also have the right to expect that parents will fulfil their responsibilities (articles 18 and 27). Clearly, parents have the primary right and responsibility to provide for the education of their children (article 28). In response to a child's special developmental needs, this education is to be holistic and a preparation for responsible adulthood (articles 28 and 29).

Similar provisions are afforded children in church law. Parents have the primary right and responsibility to do all in their power to see to the physical, social, cultural, moral and religious upbringing of their children (c. 1136). Children have a right to baptism, a Christian name and place of origin (cc. 852.1, 867, 855, 877, 101.1 and 105.1). As parents have the primary right and responsibility to provide for the education of their children (c. 793.1), children have the right to expect that parents will fulfil these obligations (cf. cc. 851, n. 2; cf. cc. 1154, 1071.1, 3 and 1689). Furthermore, the primary right and obligation for a child's Christian education belongs to parents (cc. 226.2 and 835.4). This education should be geared to fulfil a child's right to a holistic education, one that enables him/her to acquire a sense of responsibility, a correct use of freedom and prepares him/her for participation in social life (c. 795).

Finally, it should be noted that as the Convention calls upon states to assist parents in the fulfilment of their responsibilities (articles 5, 9, 10, 14, 16, 18, 22 and 27), so too church law calls upon local churches to assist parents in fulfilling parental responsibilities (cc. 776, 777, 794, 851, n. 2, 890 and 1063, n. 1).

Second avenue of promoting children's rights: protection

Children also have the right to be *protected* from certain threats to their personhood. Justice demands fundamental liberties and protection to all participants in society. If the intention of the law is to protect children, questions must be asked such as: protection from *what* harm and from *whom*?

The UN Convention is explicit regarding the harm and the perpetrator. In essence, the Convention protects children from any actions that may harm their physical, emotional, psychological or spiritual well-being. Children are to be protected from illicit kidnapping (article 11), parental abuse and neglect (article 19), economic exploitation (article 32), narcotic and psychotropic substances (article 33), sexual exploitation (article 34), abduction, sale and trafficking (article 35), torture, capital punishment (article 37), service in armed conflicts if under the age of fifteen (article

38), and other forms of exploitation that are prejudicial to their welfare (article 36). Finally, the rights of children are to be protected within the procedural law of trials (article 40).

Canon law also seeks to protect children from certain harms and their perpetrators. The law attempts to protect children from making decisions that may be harmful to their development. This is accomplished by placing the exercise of children's rights under the authority of their parents (c. 98.2). This action is intended to prevent children from making mistakes as they place acts in the church. However, the law also admits of instances in which parents may cause harm to their own children. If a parent attempts to cause serious danger of spirit or body to a child, this is a legitimate cause for the spouses to separate (c. 1153.1). Furthermore, after the separation occurs, church law requires that adequate support and education are to be provided for the welfare of the children (c. 1154).

Children are also protected from the imposition of penalties in church law. No one under sixteen is subject to a penalty for the violation of a law or precept. Conversely, however, penalties may be imposed on adults who attempt to harm children. For instance, since human life is sacred from the moment of conception, anyone who procures an abortion is subject to the penalty of excommunication, within the confines of the law (c. 1398). A cleric who sexually abuses a minor can be punished with penalties as severe as removal from the clerical state (c. 1395.2). Parents are to be punished with a censure or other just penalty if they deliberately hand their children over to be baptized or educated in a non-Catholic religion (c.1366). In each case the intention of the law is to protect children from harmful situations.

Finally, canon law attempts to protect the procedural rights of children. Children are to stand trial through the mediation of their parents (c. 1478.1). However, if the rights of the child are in conflict with the rights of a parent, the judge is to appoint a guardian to act on behalf of the child's interests (c. 1478.2). In contentious trials involving minors the judge is to appoint an advocate for the minor (c. 1478.3). Minors below the age of fourteen are not allowed to give testimony in a contentious trial because of the pressure this may place on them, but their opinions may be heard by the judge personally (c. 1550.1). Finally, time limits in procedural law do not apply if the person is a minor (c. 1646.3). In each instance the law attempts to protect the best interests of the child.

Third avenue of promoting children's rights: proclamation

An adequate child law will not only provide for children's special needs and protect them from harm, but also proclaim their rights. Children have the right to participate in decisions affecting their lives and in society as a whole. The UN Convention affords children these rights in relation to various freedoms, for instance, freedom of equality (article 2), freedom of expression of opinion and information (articles 12 and 13), freedom of thought, conscience and religion (article 14), freedom of association, privacy, honour and reputation (articles 15 and 16), the freedom to belong to a cultural and religious group (article 30), and the freedom to be children through play and recreation (article 31).

Canon law also accords children various rights as members of the Christian faithful. There is the right associated with equality. All the Christian faithful – including children – are truly equal with regard to their dignity and Christian activity (c. 208). Children have the right to acquire knowledge of Christian doctrine (cc. 229.1, 217). They have the right to express their opinion and make their spiritual needs known (cc. 212.2 and 213). They have the right to acquire a deeper knowledge of the sacred sciences (c. 229.2). They are free to form associations (cc. 215 and 216). They enjoy the right of a good reputation and privacy (c. 220). Finally, they have the right to choose their own particular state in life (c. 219).

Aside from the freedoms all the Christian faithful share in common, canon law also proclaims that children can exercise certain rights apart from the authority of their parents. Hence, in some limited instances the concept of independent rights for children does indeed disturb the context of the inviolability of the parent-child relationship. Church teaching is clear that parents have the primary right and responsibility to care for the proper development of their child. This assumes that parents and children have interests that are essentially the same. However, one must admit that there are situations in which children and parents may have identifiably separate interests, especially as children grow beyond infancy and early childhood into adolescence and young adulthood. Quite naturally, as children mature, they begin to assert their independence from their parents. Failure to recognize the multiplicity of interests involved, and the natural move toward partial independence, leads to a hesitation, if not a denial, regarding the proclamation of specific rights for children.

Canon law does not admit to this failure. It allows for the proclamation that in certain instances children may exercise their rights apart from the authority of their parents (c. 98.2). These instances include exceptions clearly stated in divine and canon law. Most exceptions are allowed after a child has attained the use of reason, presumably at the age of seven. At the age of seven a child may acquire a *quasi-domicile* of his/her own (c. 105.1); also, what is prescribed in the canons on the baptism of adults is applicable to children at this age (c. 852.1). At the age of seven one has the right to receive the sacraments of penance, eucharist (c. 914) and the anointing of the sick (c. 1004.1). In case of a spiritual matter, children of seven can act or respond without the consent of their parents (c. 1478.3).

At the age of fourteen a minor can choose to be baptized in the Latin or another ritual church (c. 111.2). If he or she had been enrolled in another ritual church at an earlier age by parents, the minor of fourteen can choose to return to the Latin Church (c. 112.1, n. 3). At fourteen, minors may be witnesses in a case before an ecclesiastical court (c. 1550.1). At sixteen, they may be sponsors for baptism or confirmation, and at seventeen they may freely enter the novitiate of a religious institute or society of apostolic life. Though the instances in which children may exercise rights apart from parental authority are limited in church law, their presence recognizes that as children mature they begin to acquire the exercise of certain rights through their own volition.

The Code of canon law does not contradict the Convention in proclaiming the evolving capacity of the child to make decisions. The Convention acknowledges the same concept in article 5 in so far as states are to '. . . respect the responsibilities, rights and duties of parents, . . ., to provide, in a manner consistent with the evolving capacities of the child, appropriate direction and guidance in the exercise by the child of the rights recognized in the present Convention'.

The Convention and canon law are compatible in so far as both provide for children's special needs, protect their welfare in harmful situations and proclaim their freedoms and rights as human beings. However, these rights must not be viewed in isolation from the family.

Respect for parental rights and family primacy

Parents: the Convention and Code

There is an understandable fear that when the rights of children are promoted in legislation the rights of parents may be diminished by the state or the church. However, such fear is unfounded ecclesially. Pope John Paul II's 1981 apostolic exhortation on the family states that the family is the basic cell of society and the subject of rights and duties before the state or any other community. The church defends the rights of the family against any usurpation by society or the state. For example, the church holds that every human person has the right to found a family and to have adequate means to support it. There is the right to the transmission of life and the education of children, as well as the right to bring up one's children in accordance with the family's own traditions and religious and cultural values. So from within a Catholic perspective, the rights of children are always to be viewed under the umbrella of the family.

Though children are afforded rights by virtue of their human dignity (not by some concession of the adult members of the human family), most children live their lives in the context of a family environment. Article 5 states plainly that states are to respect the parents and family in their child-rearing functions. This is a pivotal article for the proper implementation of the Convention. Children's rights are not to be set in contradiction to parental rights and responsibilities (unless of course there is severe parental negligence or abuse). The Convention attests to the importance of parental rights in numerous articles (nos. 7, 9, 10, 14, 16, 18, 20, 22 and 27). It also presumes the fulfilment of parental responsibilites in its canonization of parental rights. Canon law does the same.

The Holy See acceded to the Convention in its sovereign state capacity listing its declarations and reservations. These legal specifications indicated that the Holy See interprets the articles of the Convention in a way that safeguards the primary and inalienable rights of parents. This is particularly so when these rights concern education (articles 13 and 28), religion (article 14), association with others (article 15) and privacy (article 16). This is very much in keeping with the code of canon law. Canon 98.2 is clear that children are subject to the authority of their parents in the exercise of rights, unless divine law or canon law exempts children from the power of their parents. This recognition of parental prerogatives is rooted in natural law. Since parents have given life to their children, they have the primary right and obligation for their development.

Conclusion

The Holy See was one of the first states to accede to the United Nations Convention on the Rights of the Child. The presence of the Holy See at the United Nations represents the voice of the universal Roman Catholic Church (cc. 113.1 and 361). The church has the right to declare moral principles, including principles which pertain to the social order and support the fundamental rights of the human person (c. 747.2). His Excellency, Archbishop Martino, Permanent Observer of the Holy See to the United Nations, stated on the occasion of accession:

> One must always keep in mind that the rights of the child are not a concession granted by the governments or by the adult members of the human family. They are inherent in the child's nature and the purpose of legislation is to recognize and uphold them to the fullest.[2]

By acceding to the convention, the Catholic Church has demonstrated on the world stage its genuine and constant interest in the well-being of children. This interest in child advocacy is borne out in the church's legal system, which like the Convention combines nurturance and self-determination rights in a balanced perspective, thus supporting the development of healthy families.

Notes

1. There are two codes presently in use in the Roman Catholic Church: one affecting the Latin Church, the other, the Eastern Churches. For the purposes of this presentation the focus will be the 1983 *Code of Canon Law* for the Latin Church which contains 1752 canons.

2. Remarks on the occasion of accession of the Holy See to the Convention (20 April 1990).

The *Pastoral do menor* in São Paulo

Dominique Appy

The *Pastoral do menor* aims, in the light of the gospel and critical awareness, to stimulate a process which mobilizes society as a whole to transform the situation of the child and the adolescent.

Foundation

The *Pastoral do menor* was officially founded in December 1977. The Cardinal of São Paulo, Dom Paulo Evaristo Arns, invited Dom Luciano Mendès de Almeida, then bishop of the episcopal region of Belèm, an area of São Paulo, to organize and direct the *Pastoral do menor*, the aim of which was to help young people in difficulties. Before 1977 there was a movement made up of seminarians and religious who had supported a project arranged by FEBEM (Brazilian public assistance). This project, entitled 'Supervised Freedom', aimed at guiding and helping young delinquents designated by the judge.

Development

Once the team of *Pastoral do menor* had been formed, after studying the situation it modified the old project. It judged it necessary to involve the families of the young persons concerned and to bring in the community, if adolescents were to be given the best chances of being reintegrated into their milieu. The new project was called 'Assisted Community Freedom'. Community centres were founded where necessary.

During the 1980s the *Pastoral do menor* organized itself to respond to the needs of children and adolescents, the number of which did not cease to grow. In this way aid centres, homes and workshops were created. Street teachers were trained. Adoption became an option. More recently, however, in view of the problem of AIDS, which affects many young people, Fr Julio Lancelotti, co-ordinator of the *Pastoral do menor* until 1992 and now in contact with FEBEM, launched the Casa Vida project, which has had good results.

Towards the end of the 1980s, statutes on the rights of the children and adolescents for whom the *Pastoral do menor* struggles unceasingly were developed.

The social reality

The disastrous economic situation of the country, which has dramatic repercussions at a social level, and the lack of interest on the part of successive governments in developing a social policy, are the causes of the poverty and misery which have produced the great problem of children in need. A survey by the Research Institute of Applied Economics has shown that in the city of São Paulo alone, 202,022 have an income which hardly covers the basic nutrition recommended by UNO and other agencies.

In addition to the ravages caused by hunger, violence is rampant. According to the Centre for Studies Against Violence, a child is killed every three days in São Paulo. Parents are responsible for 17.8% of these crimes, and the military police for 12.8%. The Regional Centre for Maltreated Children states that around 500,000 children are maltreated by their parents in the state of São Paulo. According to the Secretariat for the Child, the Family and Social Welfare this represents a growth of 338% between 1990 and 1993.

Abuse followed by death represents 29.4% of homicides against children below the age of ten. 84% of the victims are girls. In addition to economic and emotional factors, family and urban violence drives children from their homes and puts them on the streets, where they become marginalized.

According to the Secretariat for the Child, the Family and Social Welfare, there are 4,520 children on the streets of the city of São Paulo by day and 895 by night. These are only children encountered in the street; for security reasons, abandoned houses, cars and other places where children shelter were not inspected.

The *Pastoral do menor* – constitution and function

The *Pastoral do menor* is headed by an archdiocesan co-ordinator, his assistant and a secretary as the executive team. The Pastoral is divided into six regions in six distinct areas of São Paulo: Belèm, Brasilândia, Ipiranga, Lapa, Santana and Sé. Each region is linked to an episcopal see and its projects suit the local situation. The teams which direct the projects choose appropriate activities in conjunction with the bishop, the local church or local groups.

An archdiocesan council meets each month, consisting of the executive team and two representatives of each region. Its role is:
– To finalize programmes like the preparation for the way of the cross for children during Holy Week (4,000 children come from all over São Paulo).
– To decide what to do with certain children: for example, a child with AIDS will be sent to an appropriate centre.
– To study contacts with other movements working in the same area.
– To seek to implant the statutes relating to children and adolescents in guardianship councils and legal councils (municipal and state) by introducing members of the *Pastoral do menor*.
– To struggle constantly to have the rights of children and adolescents respected. A law passed by the Brazilian people in 1990, decreed by the Congress and sanctioned by the President of the Republic, and which has been disseminated by the *Pastoral do menor*, states:

> The duty of the family, society and the state is to ensure as a priority for children and adolescents the rights to life, education, leisure, dignity, apprenticeship to a form of work, culture, respect, freedom, and family and community life (Article 227 of the Federal Constitution).

The *Pastoral do menor* considers that its mission, in addition to the help it gives to street children and adolescents, is to remind everyone how urgent it is to apply these statutes. It believes that this is possible with good will and much love.

To help children and young people in the areas of Belèm and Brasilândia there are municipal and private crèches in which members of the Pastoral work. Children with AIDS are also accepted in specialist homes there. The six regions have community centres and protective centres; four of them have workshops for apprenticeships to a profession (carpentry, mechanics, electrical engineering, recycling paper).

The Sé region already has a fairly complete structure with:
– A home for young people who are apprentices.
– A training centre where children are taught to read and write, are given psychological and educational help in a group or as individuals, and are prepared for the world of work, school and family. They are also given dental and medical checks and treatment.

– A transit home open to adolescent girls between twelve and sixteen, who are often pregnant. They learn how to live in a structured space and are taught hygiene and how to read and write and do manual work; they are also given courses in cooking. They are fed and given medical care.

The *Pastoral* houses young people who have gone through all these stages of the recuperation process successfully and have obtained employment in huts bought in the favela. These young people end up buying the houses for a token payment to the *Pastoral*.

– A country property where young people at risk are welcomed from time to time, and a teacher and some children spend weekends. In the coming months this property will be developed so that agricultural and ecological activities can begin. The rural origin of many of the children on the one hand and the stressful life of São Paulo on the other suggest that this educational project in the country will renew their links with nature, with elements vital and necessary for their lives. Drug addicts and young people at risk will be welcomed and cared for here.

Training teachers

The *Pastoral do menor* regards the training of teachers as absolutely necessary for effective work. Those recruited are often psychologists, educationalists, philosophers, religious, people who feel it their vocation to work with these children. They receive only scant remuneration for this hard work. Furthermore, because of lack of resources it is impossible to have sufficient teachers.

Each region organizes its training programme, either by bringing together the team responsible with the teachers to try to adapt theory to practice or by encouraging them to go on courses and to lectures on education. To complete this training the archdiocesan team organizes meetings with the teachers and teams of all the regions of São Paulo to share problems which arise and reflect on them.

The *Pastoral do menor* also trains volunteers, who are often students and sometimes foreigners: these join the team and support the teachers. Their training, by the local leaders, includes the history of the *Pastoral do menor*, the ethos of the Pastoral, the social and family background of children and adolescents and how to deal with young people.

The ethos of the *Pastoral do menor*

Like all pastoral work in the Catholic Church, the *Pastoral do menor* has a

Christian ethos. All the teachers choose the option of putting the gospel into practice.

While being Catholic, the *Pastoral do menor* is also ecumenical. It joins up with other groups and churches which are working and struggling just as hard to win life and citizenship for children who are excluded.

Those who work with children on the streets, in the homes, in the workshops or the community concerned, are always concerned to give them time to reflect in an informal way. A taste for life and interest in life are important values. It is not a question of making these children Catholics, but of trying to help them to discover the joy of being deeply and specially loved by God. One example of this is the sharing of food, which street children do almost instinctively. When a boy or a girl has been given some food, he or she shares it with everyone, children and teachers. And in the view of these children, pregnant girls must eat more. This Christian behaviour is worth any catechesis. The teacher intervenes only to remind them how fine the gesture is and how important for togetherness and help, and to tell them that God blesses them when they share.

The teacher and young people

Faced with the problems experienced by street children and adolescents, the *Pastoral* is seeking to create links with them in order to help them, by means of appropriate strategies and methods. When these children get to know their teachers, emotional bonds are created, along with a trust which encourages confidences. Drugs cease to be essential, and it becomes possible for the teachers to treat the problems of young people by involving them in educational activities which extend as far as developing projects for the future. The prospects of a better life take shape.

The first aim is certainly to help children to live in community in order to allow them to get to know their duties and rights as citizens better. The basic strategies for achieving this objective call for association, progress step by step, and participation. Activities and services are adapted to the stage of development and the limitations of children and young people.

Main objective

To teach them respect and help them to recognize that their group is part of a people with a culture.

Specific objects

To create real conditions so that they can reflect on the actual life they are living. To encourage moments of solidarity and sharing. To reflect with them on their attitude within the group.

Methodology

The essential basic attitude in this project is respect for young people, their values and the organization of their innermost life, respect for them as children of God.

An active and constant presence is needed. By that we understand a presence which brings the love and friendship that enable children to express themselves.

Specifically, the teachers always approach the children in groups. This happens naturally in a variety of situations, when they are cleaning shoes, playing, bathing in the public fountains, sleeping, trying to escape the police, sniffing glue or varnish, and so on. Listening is essential. A relationship of mutual trust has to be established. Sporting and artistic activities and games, the necessary care and medical treatment, often create the special bonds which allow the teachers to guide these children and give them their bearings, to the point of getting them back into society.

Who are these children?

They always come from a class in Brazilian society which is very much frowned on. Their poverty and their tender age make them doubly vulnerable and fragile. They are not wanted at home and suffer cruelty which makes them run away. And on the streets, where they think they can find a refuge, they are faced with even greater violence. They begin by begging to survive, but rarely get the help they expect. Little by little they commit petty theft and in this way become enemies of society. They match hostility with hostility, and are marginalized, becoming little savages, dirty and sullen, their heads plunged at one time or another into a bag of glue or varnish which makes them giddy and intoxicated, and eventually gives them the courage to embark on some bad act. Very soon they become the prey of adult perverts who lead them on to steal or to be prostitutes, and who use them in drug traffic. The police, though they are not fooled, take away the children and not the adults, sometimes beat them to death or shoot them. These children become feared and cursed by all society. And for many people the only solution is to get rid of them. But those who, like the teachers of the *Pastoral do menor*, have a chance to get near to these children and tame them, discover their true face. Many of them have the tender heart of a child, an often keen intelligence, immense sensitivity and artistic gifts (painting, poetry and so on). A poem by Jonathan, who is eighteen, illustrates this.

The Tears which Do Not Flow

I walk and I see a bird
feeding its young. What happiness!
The ants work with joy, day and night.
I keep walking and think of my problems,
but the tears do not flow.
I knew someone who could not walk,
who lost this right, but he is happy.
He plays, smiles, is very intelligent.
But the tears do not flow.
I see children breathing varnish and glue,
on their faces one reads sad scenes
which mark their everyday life.
But the tears do not flow.
There are many people like us, him,
them, me, who have never had father or mother
and who need the support of society.
But the tears do not flow.
I see this little girl who had a home,
a mother, but who was abused.
Today she has an arrogant smile
and shamelessly sells her body.
But the tears do not flow.
I stop midway, thinking of all
the difficulties of all, the birds
which do not work yet feed their young.
Suddenly I have understood our difficulties.
I have stopped to think 'Why?'
The tears begin to flow

What solution?

The situation of these children, adolescents, marginalized, oppressed and exploited, is a clear indication of a destructured society whose scale of social, economic and political values has been shattered. Once brought out, this reality clearly shows that the solution is to give priority to people, to their basic rights and values, and especially to justice and brotherhood.

These street children, abandoned, poor and marginal, are a great challenge to the church, society and the state. In the face of this harsh reality the National Conference of Brazilian Bishops created in 1964 the Campaign for Brotherhood, with a theme which changes every year. The theme for 1995 is the excluded, like the street children. The Campaign of Brotherhood, within the *Pastoral*, affirms the radical nature of Christian life at its two poles, faith and charity, and becomes a privileged means of living out Lent all the year, as an inspiring light and guideline for the life of the church.

If we are to reshape the ethical and cultural fabric of our society, we shall also need a special process of conversion in each one of us along with just economic demands, reassuming the liberating compromises which integrate faith. One of the most important ways forward is to seek transformation among people and in society, beginning from the child victims, putting them at the centre of our communities and our projects.

Society, the state and even more the church must never lose sight of the meaning of the words sharing and solidarity.

Translated by John Bowden

The African Synod: A Stocktaking

Maurice Cheza

The aspiration of African Christians towards an expression of faith which is rooted in their culture have become far stronger since the 1960s, as a result of political independence on the one hand and conciliar *aggiornamento* on the other.

In 1972/73, Alioune Diop (a Senegalese lay Christian, founder of *Présence africaine*) conceived the idea of bringing together the whole of the African episcopate and communicated it to the bishops of West Africa. Under the stimulus of Diop, the colloquium of the African Society for Culture (*Civilisation noire et Eglise catholique*, Abidjan, September 1977) put forward a proposal for an 'African Council'. For more than ten years this idea went the rounds among bishops and theologians, mainly in Zaire and Cameroon but also in broader authorities like SECAM (The Symposium of Episcopal Conferences of Africa and Madagascar) and EATA (Ecumenical Association of African Theologians).

Rome preferred the formula of a 'special assembly for Africa of the Synod of Bishops', more usually called 'African Synod', to this formula of a 'council' for which the bishops of Africa would have been responsible by reason of their mission as successors of the apostles. The Synod of Bishops, created by Paul VI, relates more to pontifical primacy than to episcopal collegiality: its aim is 'to aid the Roman Pontiff in his councils'.

There were several intermediate stages between the announcement of the African Synod on 6 January 1989 and the promulgation by the Pope of the apostolic exhortation *Ecclesia in Africa* (14 September 1995): the publication of the *Lineamenta* in July 1990, followed by preparatory work in Africa on the basis of the questionnaire contained in the *Lineamenta*. The working document was published in February 1993: the Pope announced that the 'working sessions' would be held in Rome, but that he would then go to Africa for a 'phase of celebration'. The Synod took place in Rome from 10 April to 8 May 1994. The first two weeks were devoted to numerous contributions by the Fathers (more than 200). According to a document from the Synod secretariat, the main subjects touched on can be classified in the following order: justice (40), inculturation (35), the laity (30), living ecclesial communities (27), dialogue (18). After the third week, work was continued along linguistic lines and led to the development of the message and some propositions: the text of the message was made public at the end of the Synod, but in principle the 64 propositions voted on by the Fathers are secret. They were intended for the Pope, in order to allow him to produce his apostolic post-synodical exhortation. Thanks to various leaks, fortunately they are known, and comparison between these propositions and the text of the exhortation reminds one of what happened at Puebla.

A stocktaking – which is always difficult to do – cannot leave out the context. This is neither solely ecclesial nor is it entirely foreseeable. The killings in Rwanda (one of the most Christianized countries in Africa) began at almost the same time as the Synod; the Pope's accident provoked strong emotions; the proximity of the Cairo Conference on questions of development and demography led the Pope to express himself strongly on this subject; the first multi-racial elections in South Africa also date from this period. Finally, as chance would have it, the question of the ordination of women in the Anglican church was at the forefront at this time: on 22 February 1994 the General Synod of the Church of England ratified the decision to ordain women. Three months later, John Paul II's apostolic letter was definitively to close the door on the ordination of women to the priesthood. In short, the three ghosts of sex, the sacred and power haunted the corridors of the African Synod, as they did many places in the church.

What has the African Synod allowed? What has it held back or prevented? There are many parameters. There is a need to analyse them and put into perspective the texts to which the Synod has given rise (preparatory documents, the speech of Cardinal Thiandoum, the contributions by the Fathers, the message, the propositions, the apostolic exhortation), the symbolic gestures (specifically liturgical) which went with it, and the contacts which it made possible. This stocktaking can only be partial.

Giancarlo Zizola described the African Synod in his book *Le Successeur*. He did so briefly, but he managed to set the assembly in its Roman context and in the framework of Vatican rivalries and manoeuvres. In his view, John Paul II 'firmly encouraged and protected the African Synod', and this synod 'defined the platform for new relations between Rome and the African church' (229).

Three major themes dominated the debates: inculturation, the sufferings of the continent and recourse to the image of the family to present the church.

Inculturation: in a few decades, the centre of gravity in the Catholic world has shifted from the north of the planet to the south. Should the Christians of the south be obliged to adopt Latin culture to live out their faithfulness to Jesus Christ and the gospel? This is one of the most serious questions that the Popes of the third millennium will have to confront, with Christian intelligence and freedom. If a centralized uniformity persists, there is a great risk of seeing the multiplication of miracles, 'inculturated' healings and all kinds of mystical groups, to the detriment of a flexible church unity.

The Synod spoke of inculturation a good deal. The doors have been half-opened. For Cardinal Thiandoum, the reporter-general, inculturation touches on all aspects of life: theology, worship and liturgy, marriage and family, health and sickness, rites of initiation, new ministries appropriated better, religious and monastic life, the veneration of ancestors. On this last point, for example, proposition 36 said: 'The veneration of ancestors is a practice which does not in any way imply their adoration. So we recommend that with due precautions so as not to diminish the true worship of God or to minimize the role of the saints, the veneration of ancestors should be allowed in appropriate ceremonies, authorized and proposed by competent authorities in the church.' The apostolic exhortation does not go so far: the veneration of Africans for their ancestors is 'in some degree a preparation for faith in the communion of saints' (no. 43), and this question must be studied in the commissions (no. 64). We can note the same retreat between the propositions and the exhortation in connection with the 'world of the spirits'. Proposition 37 said: 'To serve the faithful better, we need to preach the power of Christ over every evil spirit. We also need holy people to come to the aid of those who are afflicted by such beliefs, aided by the sacraments and the sacramentals, and also by prayers for liberation.' The exhortation only takes up the suggestions of commissions to study the issue (no. 64).

The numerous speeches at the synod on the sufferings of the continent had already been very clear. The text of the final message also contains some strong phrases. For example, 'We remind all our African brothers who have diverted public funds that they are held to account to repair the wrong done to our people' (no. 32). 'The Synod energetically denounces and condemns all the concerns for power and all kinds of interests and the idolatry of racialism which lead to fratricidal wars' (no. 36). The message also contains an appeal from the Fathers of the synod to their 'brother and sister Christians in the north', in particular in connection with the sale of arms and the weight of debt. However, some of the remarks made by the Synod seem based more on idealism and moral wishes than on a realistic social and political analysis.

The text of the apostolic exhortation goes further than the Fathers of the Synod in denouncing the evils from which Africa suffers. This is the advantage of a supra-national magisterium: it allows the local bishops, involved in the concrete problems of their country, to appeal to a doctrine which transcends their local situation. The Pope recalls the profound links 'between evangelization and human promotion, development and liberation' (no. 68). He then denounces the corruption, the diversions of public money, authoritarian and oppressive regimes, tribalism, nepotism and the thirst for power. He accuses those trafficking in arms of being accomplices in hateful crimes against humanity. The international community is called to involve itself more in the service of Africa. The International Monetary Fund and the World Bank, mentioned by name, are urged to alleviate the debts which are crushing African countries.

The theme of the church as family occupies an important place throughout the dynamic of the Synod. The members of the Christian community are united by a vital force which can be compared to that which unites the members of a family. This is an interesting theme. In developing it, the Synod wants to show that tribalism and ethnic struggles must be blurred in the face of membership of the divine family. But to what image of the family is reference being made? Isn't this a family of a patriarchal type in which the head (masculine) imposes his authority on his wife and children? Furthermore, the Pope's encouragement of 'living ecclesial communities' is related to the church as family (no. 89).

A comparison between the propositions and the apostolic exhortation is interesting on another question, that of women. Proposition 48 states: 'In numerous African societies and sometimes in the church, there are traditions and practices which deprive women of their rights and the respect that is due to them. The Synod deplores this reality. It is imperative for women to be involved to an adequate degree in the decision-making process of the church and for the church to create ministries for them and to intensify efforts to train them.' The apostolic exhortation (no. 121) no longer speaks of the failings of the church towards women, and the desire for women's ministries is replaced by: 'It is opportune for women, having received adequate training, to take part in the apostolic activity of the church at appropriate levels.'

In short, the Synod has stirred things up in an interesting way. Some commentaries have gone so far as to say that it was a step on the way to an

African council, but in grasping all its dynamic one cannot just keep to the apostolic exhortation, suggestive though that is.

The editors of the Special Column are Miklos Tomka and Willem Beuken. The content of the Special Column does not necessarily reflect the views of the Editorial Board of Concilium.

Contributors

NORBERT METTE was born in Barkhausen/Porta, Germany in 1946. After studying theology and sociology he gained a doctorate in theology, and since 1984 he has been Professor of Practical Theology at the University of Paderborn. He is married with three children, and is an Editorial Director of *Concilium*. He has written numerous works on pastoral theology and religious education, including: *Voraussetzungen christlicher Elementarerziehung*, Düsseldorf 1983; *Kirche auf dem Weg ins Jahr 2000* (with M. Blasberg-Kuhnke), Düsseldorf 1986; *Gemeindepraxis in Grundbegriffen* (with C. Bäumler), Munich and Düsseldorf 1987; *Auf der Seite der Unterdrückten? Theologie der Befreiung im Kontext Europas* (ed. with P. Eicher), Düsseldorf 1989; *Der Pastorale Notstand* (with O. Fuchs), Düsseldorf 1992.
Address: Liebigweg 11a, D 48165 Münster, Germany.

EMMANUEL NTAKARUTIMANA was born in Burundi in 1956. He studied at the major seminary of Burundi before becoming a Dominican and then continued his religious training in Nigeria, becoming a Doctor of Theology at Kinshasa Theological Faculty. At present he is working on a thesis on Zairean theology from the time of 'independence' (1960) to the time of 'democratization'. He was director of the office of evangelization for the Bishops' Conference of Burundi and is now assistant to the Master of the Dominican Order for Africa. Recent articles are 'Burundi. Une Eglise Catholique impuissante face au chemin tragique de la démocratie', *Dialogue* 180, 1995, 109–22; 'Un sinodo de los obispos para Africa; Y después?', *Misiones Extranjeras* 144, 1944, 568–80.
Address: Fraternité Saint-Dominique, BP 2690 Bujumbura, Burundi.

MARY ROSE MCGEADY was born in Hazelton, Pennsylvania and grew up in Washington, DC. In 1946 she entered the Daughters of Charity of St Vincent de Paul. She gained a BA in sociology at Emmanuel College and an MA in clinical psychology at Fordham University, and pursued doctoral studies in the same field at Fordham and the University of Massachusetts.

She began her forty-year career in human service and child care working with homeless and disturbed children and their families at Boston's Nazareth Child Care Centre. From 1958 to 1971 she served as administrator of child-care agencies in Boston; Rhinebeck, New York and New York City. In 1971 she joined Brooklyn Catholic Charities where she worked in related areas and became its Associate Executive Director in 1987. She became Provincial of the Daughters of Charity in 1981 and President of Covenant House in 1990.
Address: Covenant House, 364 W. 17th Street, New York, NY 10011–5002, USA.

DON S. BROWNING is author most recently of *Religious Thought and The Modern Psychologies* (Philadelphia 1987) and *A Fundamental Practical Theology* (Minneapolis 1991). He is also principal investigator of the Religion, Culture and Family Project, sponsored by the Lilly Endowment, Inc., which will publish during 1996–97 a 12-volume series of books on various aspects of families in American Society.
Address: The University of Chicago, The Divinity School, 1025 East 58th Street, Chicago Ill. 60637, USA.

ANTON A. BUCHER was born in Lucerne in 1960 and studied theology, educational psychology and philosophy. Since 1993 he has been Professor of Religious Education at the Catholic Theological Faculty of the University of Salzburg. His specialist areas are religious development, the dialogue between theology and psychology, and empirical research in the area of religious education.
Address: Universität Salzburg, Institut für Religionspädagogik, Universitätsplatz 1, A 5020 Salzburg, Austria.

WIM J. C. WEREN was born in Deurne, The Netherlands, in 1946 and studied theology in Haaren and Nijmegen. He gained a doctorate in theology in 1979 with a redaction-critical study *De broeders van de Mensenzoon: Mt 25, 31–46 als toegang tot de eschatologie van Mattëus*. Since 1984 he has been Professor of the Exegesis of the New Testament at Tilburg Theological Faculty. He has published articles in various collections and journals on new methods of exegesis and recently written two books, *Intertextualiteit en bijbel*, 1993, and *Mattëus*, 1994.
Address: Scheepersdijk 2, 5062 EC Oisterwijk, The Netherlands.

DIETER STEINER is theologian and pastoral psychologist who has a practice in Solothurn, Switzerland.
Address: Brühlstrasse 71, CH 4500 Solothurn, Switzerland.

URSULA PEUKERT was born in 1944. After a number of years as a teacher, she studied educational theory, sociology and theology and gained her doctorate with a work *Interaktive Kompetenz und Identität. Über den Vorrang des sozialen Lernens im Vorschulalter*, Düsseldorf 1979. After several years as an academic assistant at the University of Münster specializing in pre-school training she now lectures on the pedagogics of early childhood at the University of Hamburg.
Address: Innocentiastrasse 56, D 20144, Hamburg, Germany.

GEORG SPORSCHILL was born in 1946 in Feldkirch, Austria. Between 1964 and 1972 he studied theology, psychology and pedagogics in Innsbruck and Paris, gaining a doctorate in philosophy. He became a Jesuit in 1976 and was ordained priest in 1968. Between 1977 and 1988 he was editor of the journal *Entschluss*. He was involved in social work from 1982 in Vienna and from 1991 in Bucharest. He developed several projects for the homeless in Vienna and a project for street children in Rumania. Since 1995 he has been developing a community in a new area on the edge of Vienna. He is founder of the Scha'ul Schule, a religious-social community.
Address: Holetschekgasse 6A, 1210 Vienna, Austria.

BIRGIT JEGGLE-MERZ was born in Münster in 1960. She studied Catholic theology in Bonn and Freiburg and became academic assistant to the chair for liturgy and pastoralia in Freiburg im Breisgau. She trained for a number of years as a transactional analyst and since 1989 has been a member of the Council of Catholic Television Work with ZDF. She is active in training deacons and in adult education and is at present finishing a doctorate. She has written a number of articles on worship in the audiovisual media, celebrating worship with children and women and liturgy, and also specialist articles on pastoral liturgy and aspects of training. She has just been awarded a doctorate.
Address: Döbelstrasse 11, D 88677 Markdorf, Germany.

MICHAEL SMITH FOSTER received a Master of Divinity degree and a Masters of Arts degree in theology from St John's Seminary, Boston, Massachusetts, USA in 1980. He also received a Licentiate in canon law from The Catholic University of America, Washington, DC in 1989 and a

doctorate in canon law from the same university in 1994. His canonical area
of expertise is child advocacy. His doctoral dissertation is entitled 'The
Promotion of the Canonical Rights of Children in Situations of Divorce
and Remarriage'. He has served as a judge on the Boston Metropolitan
Tribunal since 1989. He has held the same position on the Boston
Provincial Court of Appeals since 1990. He was appointed Associate
Judicial Vicar of the Metropolitan Tribunal in 1994. His articles include:
'The Role of Auxiliary Bishops', *The Jurist* 51, 1991, 423–30; 'When
Churches Close', *Liturgy* 8, 1990, 71–5; 'The Violation of a Church
(Canon 121)', *The Jurist* 49, 1989, 693–703.

Address: The Metropolitan Tribunal, One Lake Street, Brighton MA
02135–3800, USA.

DOMINIQUE APPY is a nurse and a member of the Sé Regional Council of
Pastoral do menor in São Paulo.
Address: Rua Lotario Lutz 148, São Paulo 04645060, Brazil.

Members of the Advisory Committee for Practical Theology

Directors

Maureen Junker-Kenny	Dublin	Ireland
Norbert Mette	Münster	Germany

Members

Alberto Antoniazzi	Belo Horizonte	Brazil
José Arguello	Managua	Nicaragua
Don F. Browning	Chicago	USA
Fernando Castillo	Santiago	Chile
Casiano Floristán	Madrid	Spain
Ottmar Fuchs	Bamberg	Germany
Norbert Greinacher	Tübingen	Germany
Thomas Groome	Boston	USA
Frans Haarsma	Nijmegen	The Netherlands
Ferdinand Heselaars Harono	Jogjakarta	Indonesia
Joseph Hochstaffl	Paderborn	Germany
François Houtart	Louvain-la-Neuve	Belgium
Leo Karrer	Fribourg	Switzerland
Andreas Kim	Seoul	South Korea
Hubert Lepargneur OP	São Paulo SP	Brazil
Jean-Guy Nadeau	Montreal	Canada
Emmanuel Ntakarutimana	Budjumbura	Africa
Wladislaw Piwowarski	Lublin	Poland
Rosemary Radford Ruether	Evanston, Ill.	USA
Sidbe Semporé	Cotonou	Benin
Hermann Steinkamp	Münster	Germany
Paolo Suess	São Paulo	Brazil
Urbano Zilles	Porto Alegre	Brazil

Directors-Counsellors – cont.

Jürgen Moltmann	Tübingen	Germany
Mercy Amba Oduyoye	Princeton	USA
John Panagnopoulos	Athens	Greece
Aloysius Pieris SJ	Gonawala-Kelaniya	Sri Lanka
James Provost	Washington, DC	USA
Giuseppe Ruggieri	Catania	Italy
Christoph Theobald SJ	Paris	France
Miklós Tomka	Budapest	Hungary
David Tracy	Chicago, IL	USA
Marciano Vidal CSSR	Madrid	Spain
Knut Walf	Nijmegen	The Netherlands

General Secretariat: Prins Bernardstraat 2, 6521 A B Nijmegen, The Netherlands
Manager: Mrs E. C. Duindam-Deckers

Concilium Subscription Information
- outside North America

Individual Annual Subscription (1996 six issues): £30.00

Institution Annual Subscription (1996 six issues): £40.00

Airmail subscriptions: add £10.00

Individual issues: £8.95 each

New subscribers please return this form:
for a two-year subscription, double the appropriate rate

1996 *Concilium* subscriptions   ☐   £30.00   ....
            (for individuals)

1996 *Concilium* subscriptions   ☐   £40.00   ....
            (for institutions)

For airmail postage outside Europe   ☐   + £10.00   ....
(optional) please add £10.00

                                Total   . . . .

I wish to subscribe for one/two years as an individual/institution
(delete as appropriate)

Name . . . .

Address . . . .

. . . .

. . . . Postcode . . . .

I enclose a cheque for .... made payable to SCM Press Ltd

Please charge my Access/Visa/Mastercard No ..../............./............./.............

Signature .... Expiry Date ....

Please send this form to:
SCM Press Ltd (Concilium) 9-17 St Albans Place London N1 0NX
Credit card telephone orders on: 0171-359 8033 Fax: 0171-359 0049

CONCILIUM

The Theological Journal of the 1990s

Now available from Orbis Books

Founded in 1965 and published six times a year, *Concilium* is a world-wide journal of theology. Its editors and essayists encompass a veritable 'who's who' of theological scholars. Not only the greatest names in Catholic theology, but exciting new voices from every part of the world, have written for this unique journal.

Concilium exists to promote theological discussion in the spirit of Vatican II, out of which it was born. It is a catholic journal in the widest sense: rooted firmly in the Catholic heritage, open to other Christian traditions and the world's faiths. Each issue of *Concilium* focusses on a theme of crucial importance and the widest possible concern for our time. With contributions from Asia, Africa, North and South America, and Europe, *Concilium* truly reflects the multiple facets of the world church.

Now available from Orbis Books, *Concilium* will continue to focus theological debate and to challenge scholars and students alike.